Instant Bible Lessons

Gospel Illusions

Object Lessons You Can Do!

Randy Burtis

Dedicated to all the faithful Sunday school and children's ministry workers. And to my wife and two daughters. God has blessed me to teach his precious ones and use these simple tricks to expand his kingdom.

Glory to God!

Instant Bible Lessons: Gospel Illusions: Object Lessons YOU Can Do!

ISBN: 978-1-62862-816-6
RoseKidz® Reorder #R50019
RELIGION/Christian Ministry/Children

Printed in the United States of America
Printed May 2019

ConTENTS

INTRODUCTION

When I started teaching children over thirty-five years ago, I vowed my lessons would be exciting and enjoyable for my students. We are teaching God's Word! As Young Life founder Jim Rayburn famously said, "We believe it is sinful to bore kids with the gospel."

IMPORTANCE OF VISUAL LEARNING

We learn more easily if we can connect an abstract concept with something visual or concrete. Flashcards, pictures, and objects help us to teach and also to learn. Gospel illusions (a.k.a. "magic tricks") function in the same way—to the enth degree!

I have been doing gospel illusions for over twenty-five years. I love it! And so do the kids I teach. I combine an illusion with a Bible story or spiritual truth to create a teaching moment that engages every kid—and all the adults—in the class.

I have compiled some illusions that:

- will capture the attention of your kids

- won't cost you a bundle of money

- will teach kids about spiritual matters

> ILLUSIONS ARE JUST TOOLS TO HELP YOU DELIVER THE TRUTH IN AN ENGAGING WAY. THE FOCUS SHOULD ALWAYS BE ON BIBLICAL TRUTH.

Although the illusions given here won't take months of practice, take time to practice so that your actions are smooth. You can then focus on the lesson you want to teach. Illusions are just tools to help you deliver the truth in an engaging way. The focus should always be on biblical truth.

Remember: the trick is secondary! In order to keep the illusion in its right place, practice both the method and the presentation around it so that both are well rehearsed. A poorly executed illusion will take away from the message. If you are so focused on "getting the trick right" your teaching will suffer.

Also, an illusion isn't always the best option for every lesson, so don't try to force a fit. Illusions are just one of many tools a teacher has at their disposal. A good teacher uses the right tool at the right time and doesn't rely on just one tool all the time. Using a variety of presentation approaches helps kids stay engaged!

SHHHH! IT'S A SECRET.

Naturally, people will ask how the illusion was done. It is important to make clear that you don't have supernatural "magic" powers, but I strongly encourage you to keep the actual techniques a secret. Kids may THINK they need to know how the illusion works, but when they find out they are usually disappointed. On the other hand, by keeping it secret, kids will continue to have the fun of being amazed.

As you read some of the explanations YOU may be a bit disillusioned (see what I did there?). You may wonder if the illusion is too simple to wow them. But I assure you, the illusions are well-tested and the effects will deliver.

When kids beg you to tell them, "How did you do it?" Borrow my answer:

> *That is the wrong question, the right question is, WHY did I do it? And the answer is, to grab your attention so you take in the amazing truths from God's Word!*

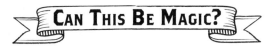

CAN THIS BE MAGIC?

There can be some concern over the use of the word *magic*. I steer clear of that word in church because these illusions are not the same "magic" that the Bible refers to as evil in 2 Chronicles 33:6. This reference is speaking out against interacting with the supernatural and evil spirits.

A gospel illusion is an object lesson with a twist, a trick, a natural effect that is hiding the method that makes it happen. There are no supernatural powers involved. I also tell the kids that what I'm doing is a fun trick, hand-is-faster-than-the-eye stuff.

Some may say we need to steer clear of even these tricks because it can give the appearance that we are using supernatural powers. To that I usually respond by saying:

> *Just because you can't immediately explain something doesn't mean you have to default to it being something it isn't.*

> *Science, until the natural laws around it are discovered, can appear to be supernatural. Once we understand the natural law that God created around that particular science effect, we then know how it works, but to the one who doesn't know that, it can seem almost magical. That doesn't make it magic.*

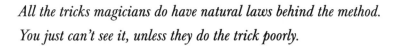

All the tricks magicians do have natural laws behind the method.
You just can't see it, unless they do the trick poorly.

I might also offer this illustration:

If a person from a couple hundred years ago saw a moving car, they would not be able to explain how it works. They could very well think a supernatural force was at work. We know the secret is gas and an engine, etc. The inability of that person to understand the technology and science behind the internal combustion engine doesn't make the car magic.

OBJECT LESSONS BASICS

Using these illusions is simply using a theatre art, an object to illustrate. Jesus used objects to help illustrate spiritual truths and make spiritual concepts more relatable.

MAKE IT YOUR OWN

As you read this book, know that there can be multiple presentation angles for each illusion and multiple verses and Bible stories to which they might apply. I encourage you to be creative and write your own presentations for the various illusions.

PRACTICE MAKES PERFECT

Have someone you trust be practice eyes for you. Once you have rehearsed it, demonstrate it to them so that you get comfortable doing the illusion and teaching in front of others. Ask them to give you feedback on how well you presented it.

Don't get discouraged or give up on an illusion if they spot the method. Ask them what they actually SAW. There are two reasons to ask what they saw:

1. You can narrow down what aspect of the illusion needs more practice.

2. They might just be guessing methods and happen to be right.
    Remember: You don't have to confirm any of these guesses!

Also, during your presentation, kids may shout out ways they think the illusion works. Even if they manage to hit the right method, it is often just a lucky guess.

There are a couple of approaches you can take to address kids calling out during an illusion:

- You can tell them to talk to you afterwards and share what they think.

- You can encourage them to keep their guesses to themselves during the presentation so that it doesn't distract others.

- You can nod and smile and say, "I told you it was all tricks, now just enjoy it. Remind me, what is this illusion trying to teach us?"

Turning it back to them helps remind everyone that the illusion is secondary, the Bible truth it illustrates is primary. THAT is what they need to know!

Have fun presenting these. Your kids will also have fun AND they will learn along the way.

Enjoy!

Randy Burtis

HOW TO USE THIS BOOK

Each object lesson begins with some helpful information.

- **Difficulty Rating**—uses a star rating to rank the difficulty of the illusion from one to five. Also gives a brief explanation of the rating. (See "The Difficulty Rating Explained" on p. 10.)

- **Effect**—gives a brief description of what the audience will see when you do the illusion.

- **Connection**—provides a biblical context for the illusion.

- **Scripture**—lists the verse or verses used in the script for each illusion. Do not limit the use of the illusion to the specified verse(s). Feel encouraged to make your own connections and use the illusions to illustrate other biblical truths. For some illusions, there are "additional Scriptures" that could be used to make your own connections.

- **Materials**—lists everything you need to perform the illusion.

PREPARATION

The Preparation section explains whatever you need to prepare ahead of time. Helpful photographs take you step-by-step.

SCRIPT

The script spells out what to say and do as you perform the illusion. It is very important that you practice the illusion until you are comfortable with the actions as well as the script.

GOSPEL ILLUSIONS

DIFFICULTY RATING EXPLAINED

Each effect is rated in difficulty from one to five stars with one star being the easiest and five stars being the most difficult. The rating reflects two primary criteria with a number of variables involved in each with one star being the easiest and five stars being the most difficult.

1. ***The Difficulty of the Presentation***

    All the illusions in this book are completely doable for anyone who works with kids. Some just require more practice. For example Chapter 1: Wordless has a very easy method. Chapter 38: Transformed is the most difficult. Whether easy or difficult, they ALL require some practice!

2. ***The Difficulty of the Preparation***

    This could be presentation preparation or prop preparation. For example, Chapter 26: Multiplying Money is a simple presentation, but the preparation of the prop takes time.

BOTTOM LINE

Read through each illusion and don't let the rating rattle you. Prepare ahead of time and you will be able to master any illusion in this book. And more importantly, you will be impressing God's Word upon the minds and hearts of your kids.

A NOTE ABOUT APPROPRIATE AGE

Generally, in order to enjoy and understand the concepts presented, your audience should be kindergarten-aged or older. Illusions are GREAT for teaching adults!

CHAPTER 1

WORDLESS

Difficulty Rating: ★★ Some craft preparation required.

Effect: Five loose colored pages mysteriously become a wordless book.

Connection: This illusion helps explain the concept of sin and the need for a Savior.

Scripture: Romans 3:23; 5:8; 6:23; 10:9–10

MATERIALS

- Double-Walled Bag (see p. 12)

- Wordless book (purchased, or assembled using directions on p. 13)

- 5 sheets of colored paper, one in each of the following colors: gold or yellow, black or other dark color, white, red, and green

PREPARATION

1. Make a double-walled bag using the instructions on page 12.

2. Put the wordless book in the main section of the double-walled bag. Fold the bag flat.

3. Keep the five separate sheets of colored paper outside the double-walled bag.

4. Practice the illusion.

SCRIPT

(*Hold up gold or yellow sheet of paper.*) Gold or yellow speaks to the street of gold in Heaven and how God wants us to be there with him because he loves us so much (see Romans 5:8). (*Place sheet into the secret pocket in the bag. Repeat with each of the five colors, after you've explained their meaning.*)

The dark color (*Hold up dark sheet of paper. Be sure to say "dark." We don't want to equate "black" with sin.*) represents sin that separates us from the relationship God wants to have with us (see Romans 3:23).

Red (*Hold up red sheet.*) represents the blood of Jesus shed so our sins could be forgiven (see Romans 6:23).

(*Hold up white sheet.*) When our sins are forgiven, our spirits are made clean before God (see Romans 10:9–10).

The green (*Hold up green sheet.*) represents growing. The gospel isn't about the future and where we go when we die, it is about a relationship NOW with God and we, like a plant, want to grow. We grow by praying, reading God's Word, going to church, and telling others about Jesus.

Now if we put all this together, what have we got? (*Reach into the bag and pull out the completed book, showing it to the audience and flipping through the pages. Show the bag empty by tipping it upside down while your hand holds the secret pocket closed. You can also angle the opening toward the audience as your hand will be concealing the opening of the secret pocket.*)

ALTERNATE IDEA

Another more dramatic way to show the bag empty is to hold the bag with the double wall towards yourself and then rip the front wall, the one furthest from you, showing the inside of the bag and revealing the book. Then discard the bag. Remember to get the single colored sheets out of the secret pocket before recycling the bag.

HOW TO MAKE A DOUBLE-WALLED BAG

A double-walled bag contains a hidden layer that conceals a secret object or objects. There will be several effects you can do with a double-walled bag.

Once you understand the construction, you can make double-walled bags from different types of bags. Use a lunch bag for the "Wordless" illusion (p. 11). Use a green gift bag when you do "Fishers of Men" (p. 17). Changing the color and type of bag will keep your audience guessing. They won't think anything is up with the bag if you don't use the same bag all the time.

MATERIALS

- 2 brown paper bags
- glue

DIRECTIONS

1. Cut out the sides and bottom from a bag.

2. Fold the sides over (image a).

A

3. Apply glue to the sides and bottom of the pocket.

4. Carefully insert the pocket into the bag and press the pocket in place. Wait for it to dry (image b).

B

5. With your hand, cover the edge with the pocket. Display the empty portion of the bag to the audience.

HOW TO MAKE A WORDLESS BOOK

A wordless book is a five-color booklet that is used to illustrate the gospel. Each color in the book explains an aspect of the gospel. There are lots of verses you can tie into each point.

MATERIALS

- 5 sheets of colored paper; one each in gold or yellow, black or other dark color, white, red, and green

- glue

DIRECTIONS

1. Fold the sheets in half.

2. The green sheet will be the outside cover. Glue one side of the gold or yellow cardstock to the inside front green cover.

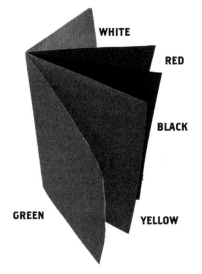

3. Glue the remaining side of the gold or yellow sheet to one side of the dark sheet.

4. Glue the remaining side of the dark sheet to one side of the red sheet.

5. Glue the remaining side of the red sheet to one side of the white sheet.

6. Glue the remaining side of the white sheet to the inside of the green cover.

CHAPTER 2

JELLY-BEAN GOSPEL

Difficulty Rating: ★★★ Requires a tricky move that needs practice.

Effect: An empty box produces bags of jelly beans.

Connection: Each bag of jelly beans represents a color from the wordless book. Use this illusion to present the gospel.

Scripture: Romans 3:23; 5:8; 6:23; 10:9–10.

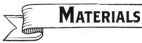

MATERIALS

- jelly beans in yellow, black, white, red, green

- snack-sized resealable plastic bags

- scissors

- fishing line

- shoe box with lid

- transparent tape

Optional

- purple jelly beans

- blue jelly beans

PREPARATION

1. Separate the jelly beans into colors (yellow, black, white, red, green, and optional purple or blue), placing each color in a separate snack bag.

2. Cut a few inches of fishing line, one for each jelly-bean bag. Tape a length of fishing line to the top of each jelly-bean bag. In the images, ribbon is used instead of fishing line for illustration purposes.

3. Attach the other end of each length of fishing line to a long inside rim of the shoe box's lid. The bags of beans are taped to hang behind the lid. Make sure when the bag hangs down, it can't be seen from the other side of the lid (image a).

4. Place lid on box so that the bags of beans hang down inside the box (image b).

Optional: Prepare additional bag(s) with purple and/or blue jelly beans.

5. Practice the illusion.

Here we have an ordinary shoe box. Here is its ordinary lid. (*Hold shoe box so that the end with the taped bags is closest to you. In one smooth motion, lift the lid and move it forward to the edge of the box. The bags should fall into the box, allowing you to tip the lid towards the audience, casually showing the audience there is with apparently nothing attached to the lid. See image c.*)

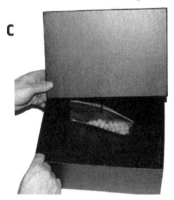

C

Here is the ordinary box. (*Flip the inside of the lid towards yourself and then raise it above the box. The bags of beans will rest against the inside of the lid, out of view of the audience. See image d.*)

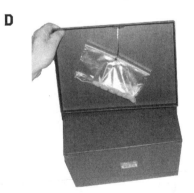

D

IMAGE D SHOWS THE PRESENTER'S VIEW. THE AUDIENCE WILL SEE THE INSIDE OF THE EMPTY BOX.

(*Tip the empty box forward to show audience the box is empty. See image e.*) But I'm going to use this ordinary box to tell you about an EXTRAORDINARY thing God did for us. (*Return box to its normal position and lower the lid as shown in image f.*)

E

F

We're going to see something amazing that will remind us of something even MORE amazing. God loves us and made a plan for us to be with him forever! (*Choose a volunteer to assist you.*)

REVEAL TWO JELLY-BEAN BAGS AT A TIME SO THE REPEATED ACTIONS OF SHOWING THE BOX EMPTY THEN HAVING BEANS APPEAR DOESN'T GET BORING, AND KEEPS YOUR GOSPEL PRESENTATION MOVING ALONG. OR CONSIDER SETTING UP INDIVIDUAL BOXES WITH ONE COLOR OF JELLY BEANS IN EACH BOX.

Reach in to pull out and reveal bag of yellow jelly beans. As you explain the meaning of the color, secretly remove fishing line if it stuck to bag when you removed it. Hand bag to volunteer to hold up. Repeat for each bag of jelly beans.) Yellow speaks to the street of gold in Heaven and how God wants us to be there with him because he loves us so much (see Romans 5:8).

The dark color (*Reveal bag of black jelly beans. Be sure to say "dark." We don't want to equate "black" with sin.*) represents sin that separates us from the relationship. God wants to have with us (see Romans 3:23). Red (*Reveal bag of red jelly beans.*) represents the blood of Jesus shed so our sins could be forgiven (see Romans 6:23).

(*Reveal bag of white jelly beans.*) When our sins are forgiven, our spirits are made clean before God (see Romans 10:9–10).

The green (*Reveal bag of green jelly beans.*) represents growing. The gospel isn't about the future and where we go when we die, it is about a relationship NOW with God and we, like a plant, want to grow. We grow by praying, reading God's Word, going to church, and telling others about Jesus.

Optional

(*Reveal bag of purple jelly beans.*) Purple is the color of royalty. When we ask God to forgive our sin and make us a member of his family, God forgives us and makes us a member of his royal family. We are the children of God!

(*Reveal bag of blue jelly beans.*) Blue represents the water of baptism. The Bible often compares washing with water to being cleansed from our sin by God's forgiveness. When we get baptized, we are showing the world that we've been forgiven by God and are followers of Jesus.

ENRICHMENT IDEA

Send home with each child a snack bag with a mix of jelly beans along with a handout explaining the meanings of the different colors.

ALTERNATE IDEA

Use this method as a fun way to introduce anything that can fit inside of the box. Consider using some of the items from another Bible story and producing them from the box at appropriate moments as you tell the story.

CHAPTER 3

FISHERS OF MEN

Difficulty Rating: ★★ Some craft preparation required.

Effect: An empty "net" suddenly fills with a bunch of fish!

Connection: Use this illusion with a lesson about Jesus calling his disciples to be fishers of men. It could also be used with the story of the miraculous catch of fish in John 21.

Scripture: Luke 5:1–11, Isaiah 43:10

MATERIALS

- Bible with Scripture references marked

- Double-Walled Bag (see page 12)

- paper cut-outs of fish (purchased or prepared ahead of time), one or more for each child

- bowl

- pen or pencil, one for each child

PREPARATION

1. Put the fish in the secret pocket of the double-walled bag.

2. Fold the bag flat.

3. Practice the illusion.

SCRIPT

(*Read Luke 5:1–5 aloud. After reading verse five, hold your hand over the opening to the secret pocket and display the empty portion of bag.*) Let's pretend this is our net. See? Just like the fishing net in the story, this is empty.

(*Read verses six and seven. Turn the "net" upside down and let all the fish come out. Try to aim for the fish to land in the bowl. Finish reading to the end of verse eleven.*)

Christians are fishers of men. This means we are to tell others about Jesus. There are at least three ways we can be fishers of men:

The first is by using our words as a "hook" to tell others about God.

The second way is through our actions. "'You are my witnesses, O Israel!' says the LORD. 'You are my servant'" (Isaiah 43:10). As a follower of Christ, you have these two jobs—witness and servant. Being God's witnesses means we know the "talk"—what God has instructed us to do. When the verse says we are God's servant, it means we do what he says. In other words, we "walk the talk."

We can be either good or bad witnesses and good or bad servants. Which do you think will be more effective as a way to tell others about God? Through our words or through our actions? (*Children respond.*)

The third way we can fish for men is by praying for those who don't know God. (*Give each child a fish and pen or pencil. Children write down the name of a "fish"—someone they want to see become a member of God's family. Children take their fish home as a reminder to pray, talk, and walk to be a good witness to that person.*)

NOTHING IS IMPOSSIBLE

Difficulty Rating: ★

Effect: A large coin somehow fits through a small hole.

Connection: Illustrates that God makes all things possible.

Scripture: Mark 10:25–27

MATERIALS

- Bible with verse reference marked

- quarter

- penny

- sheet of paper or index card

- pencil

- scissors

PREPARATION

1. Trace the penny in the center of the paper or index card.

2. Cut out circle (image a).

A

3. Practice the illusion.

SCRIPT

(*Show the paper and the quarter to the audience.*) From time to time, we might think a situation is impossible for anyone—even God. But always remember that nothing is impossible for God. God is omnipotent. Say that word with me. (*Lead children to repeat "omnipotent."*) The word omnipotent means "all powerful." All God had to do was speak, and the world, and everything in it, was created. There is no one as powerful as God and there is nothing he cannot do, no matter how impossible it may seem.

(*Hold up the paper and the penny and the quarter.*) Look how much larger the quarter is than the hole in this paper. It would be impossible for the coin to fit through the hole without tearing the paper, right? (*Children respond.*) Huh. In Mark 10:27, the Bible reminds us that "Everything is possible with God." Repeat that verse with me. (*Lead children to repeat the verse.*) Well, let's see.

(*Fold the paper in half lengthwise and drop the coin through the fold. See image b.*)

B

(*Grab the bottom edge on each side and pull up and on an angle. The coin will now slide through the hole and fall out. See image c.*)

C

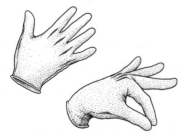

Make this a craft project.

- Children print "Everything is possible with God" on a sheet of paper or index card.

- Trace a penny in the center of the paper or index card.

- Cut out the circle.

- Children take the paper home to practice with their quarter.

Or you could buy a bunch of plastic coins from the dollar store and give one to each child to take home with the paper.

Use this script and instead of fitting a quarter through a small hole, fit your body through an index card. Use the diagram shown in image d and search online for "How to fit your body through an index card."

D

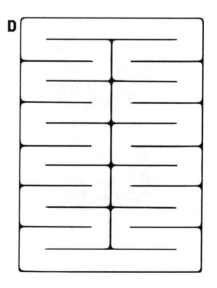

One Hand

Difficulty Rating: ★★ You need to remember the right pattern of picking up the coins.

Effect: Even though you evenly pick up coins, you end up having two more coins in one hand than the other.

Connection: Illustrates the biblical admonition not to boast when giving to the needy and "don't let your left hand know what your right hand is doing."

Scripture: Matthew 6:1–4

MATERIALS

- Bible with verse reference marked

- 7 coins of the same value

PREPARATION

Just practice!

SCRIPT

We are told in Matthew that when we give we shouldn't give in a way that others know how much we are giving. Jesus said that the left hand shouldn't know what the right hand is giving. (*Read Matthew 6:1–4 aloud.*) Watch this demonstration to help you remember this important lesson.

(*Show the seven coins, laying them on a table.*) Here we have some coins. Let's count how many there are. (*Lead children to count along with you.*)

I will put one in each hand. (*Put one coin in each hand. Close hands and turn them palm down.*)

How many are left? That's right. There are five coins on the table.

Now each hand will take a turn picking up one coin. That way everything is fair and even. (*Starting with your RIGHT hand pick up one of the coins. Use your thumb and first fingers to grab a coin and "fold" it into your hand. This way you are not opening your hand showing what each hand actually holds. Next, pick up a coin with your left hand. Go back and forth until all the coins are picked up.*)

I'm going to put five coins back on the table. But I want to keep things fair and even, so I'll go back and forth with each hand. (*Keep your closed hands palm down. Start with your LEFT hand and lay a coin on the table. Simply reverse the same movement/action you did to put a coin IN your hand, only this time you are fishing a coin OUT. Then lay one from the RIGHT hand, continue back and forth until there are five coins on the table.*)

(*It would seem that you have one coin in each hand. Actually, you should now have two coins in your right hand and none in your left hand.*) That was fair, right? Right! Each hand will now take turns and pick up one coin at a time. (*With your RIGHT hand, pick up a coin from the table and repeat with your left hand, continue until all the coins are off the table. You will have five coins in your right hand and two coins in the left hand.*)

Both hands gave evenly right? Actually . . . no. You see the hands didn't know what the other was giving and neither did your eyes!

(*Turn hands palms up and reveal the coins.*)

CHAPTER 6

ON YOUR HEAD

Difficulty Rating: ★★ You need to remember the right order of the folds.

Effect: A dollar bill turns itself upside down.

Connection: Illustrates the biblical truth, "the love of money is the root of all kinds of evil."

Scripture: 1 Timothy 6:6–12

MATERIALS

- Bible with verse reference marked

- paper bill of any denomination

PREPARATION

How do you get to Carnegie Hall? **Practice!**

SCRIPT

Many people live their lives pursuing one thing: MONEY. (*Show bill right-side up as in image a. All images are from the perspective of the performer.*) They believe by having lots of money they will be happy.

A

With a lot of money, they think they can do whatever they want and get whatever they wish. (*Fold bill in half. Left side folded over to the right as in image b.*)

B

But you know, no matter how much money you have . . . (*Fold the top half down towards you. See image c.*)

C

Money can't make you truly happy or content. (*Fold the left side to the front as in image d.*)

D

The sad thing is that a love for money leads you into doing evil destructive things. (*Let the front unfold and spring open. See image e.*)

E

People will start to lie, cheat, even steal to get more and more money. (*Unfold the FRONT to the top. See image f.*)

F

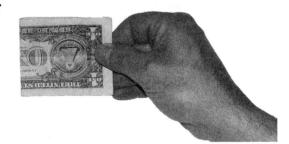

These destructive things can turn your life upside down. (*Unfold the front right to the left showing the bill turned upside down. See image g.*)

G

The Bible tells us how to turn things right-side up again by focusing on growing in Jesus and following his example. (Read 1 Timothy 6:6–12 aloud.)

CHAPTER 7

COMPLETE IN CHRIST

Difficulty Rating: ★

Effect: Three paper loops are cut. The first makes two separate loops, the second makes the loops linked together and the third turns into one big loop.

Connection: Illustrates how our sin separates us from God, and how his gift of salvation unites us with him.

Scripture: Isaiah 59:2; Ephesians 2:8–9; 1 Corinthians 6:17

MATERIALS

- Bible with Scripture references marked

- scissors

- glue or transparent tape

- 3 strips of newspaper, each approximately 3 inches wide and the width of the newspaper

> BLACK PAPER WAS USED FOR ILLUSTRATIVE PURPOSES, BUT THE ILLUSION IS MORE EFFECTIVE WITH NEWSPAPER.

PREPARATION

1. Glue or tape the first strip of paper into a loop as you normally would (image a). **Note:** Your loops will be larger than illustrated. This will make the twists less noticeable, easier to cut, and the loop easier for your class to see.

A

2. Before gluing or taping the second strip into a loop, make two twists in it (image b).

B

3. The third has one twist in it (image c).

C

4. Practice the illusion.

SCRIPT

The first loop of paper demonstrates to us what sin has done to our relationship with God. *(Pinch a part of the loop and cut a slit. Insert scissors in the loop and cut through the loop lengthwise until you are back to the start of the loop. See image d. The loops separate.)*

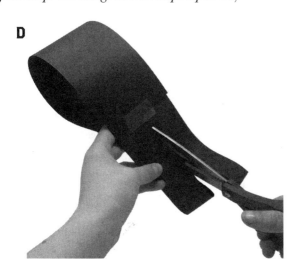

D

Sin has separated us from God. (*Read Isaiah 59:2.*)The second loop (*Show loop with two twists. As you continue speaking, cut the second loop in the same way you did the first. You will end up with the linked loops.*) shows us how we have tried to bridge the gap between ourselves and God. This represents how we have tried on our own to be complete. People have tried religion, good works, science, and everything under the sun to fill the God-shaped need that is in their life.

Now there is nothing wrong with any of the things I mentioned. They are LINKED to how we become complete, but the essential element is missing (*Show third loop with one twist.*) The third loop shows us the answer. We can be complete when we put our faith, our trust in Jesus Christ, and not in ourselves or our works.

(*Read Ephesians 2:8–9 as you cut the third loop in the same way you did the first two. You will end up with one larger loop.*)

When we accept God's gift of salvation, we are made complete. In 1 Corinthians 6:17, the Bible tells us "The person who is joined to the Lord is one spirit with him."

Difficulty Rating: ★

Effect: Pepper amazingly flees from the touch of a finger.

Connection: Represents how God's presence will cause all evil to flee.

Scripture: Matthew 5:13–15, James 4:7

MATERIALS

- Bible with Scripture references marked

- shallow white bowl or plate deep enough to hold water

- water

- dishwashing liquid

- salt

- ground pepper

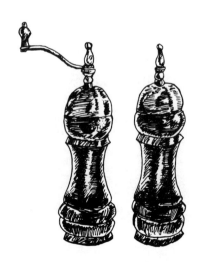

PREPARATION

1. Secretly place a drop of dishwashing liquid on your index finger.

2. Pour water into bowl or plate.

3. Practice the illusion.

SCRIPT

The Bible tells us we are to be the salt of the world. (*Pour some salt in the water. Read Matthew 5:13–15 aloud.*) God wants us to be like salt and light so that we can make a positive difference in the world.

However, God's enemy, the devil, wants to stop us. He doesn't want Christians to be like salt and light. There are all kinds of ways we can be stopped. We might give in to temptation to sin. We might not trust in God. Maybe we don't tell others about Jesus. This pepper will represent all the things that can stop God's plans. (*Pour pepper in the bowl. Dip a finger that DOES NOT have the dishwashing liquid into the bowl to show that the only thing that happens is you might get some pepper on your finger.*)

God is always with us and with him we have victory. It tells us in James 4:7 to resist the devil and he will flee. (*Dramatically.*) Devil, go! (*Dip the finger with dishwashing liquid on it in the center of the water. The pepper will move away from the finger to the edge of the bowl.*)

Now just because God has given us this power and authority this doesn't mean we go looking to pick a fight with the devil. God gives us this authority so we don't have to fear and know we can have victory when the devil tries to tempt us.

When we are tempted to sin, we don't have rely on our own strength; but instead, ask God to help us. With his help, we can send the Devil and his temptations on the run!

ALTERNATE IDEA

Ahead of time arrange to share the secret with a volunteer. Have them practice the illusion. It's not only to adults that God gives the authority and power to resist temptation. God gives that same authority and power to everyone in his family!

CHAPTER 9

HEAR THE WORD

Difficulty Rating: ★★★ Arts and craft preparation.

Effect: A ribbon is threaded through a paper bag. Paper hearts are dropped into the bag and one heart attaches itself to the ribbon.

Connection: Demonstrates a heart pierced by hearing God's Word. This is a great illusion for preparing children to carefully listen to an upcoming Bible story.

Scripture: Hebrews 4:12

MATERIALS

- Bible with verse reference marked

- Double-Walled Bag (p. 12)

- several paper hearts

- pencil

- 2- to 3-inch finishing nail (nail with no flat head)

- 6- to 8-inch length of curling ribbon

- transparent tape

Optional

- letter opener or small sword

PREPARATION

1. Make a Double-Walled Bag as described on page 12.

2. Put one of the hearts in the secret pocket of your double-walled bag. (See image a.)

Note: In the photo, one side of the bag has been cut away so that you can see the placement of the heart in the secret pocket.

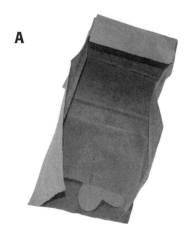

A

3. Place a small pencil dot on the outside wall of the paper bag so you know where to poke the nail through later (image b).

B

PENCIL MARK EXAGGERATED FOR ILLUSTRATIVE PURPOSES. THE MARK SHOULD BE SUBTLE.

4. Fold bag flat.

5. Tape one end of 6- to 8-inch length of curling ribbon to the blunt end of the nail.

6. Practice the illusion.

SCRIPT

In Hebrews 4:12 we are told that God's Word is sharper than a double-edged sword and its target is the human heart. (*Show the paper hearts.*)

The Bible has a message that is for every heart and every situation. God wants everyone to hear and obey it, allowing it to pierce their heart and change their lives.

(*Take the nail with the ribbon and shove it through the wall of the bag and secretly through the hidden heart. Use the pencil mark you made during Preparation. Poke it through the other side of the paper bag so the ribbon is strung through both walls. See image c.*)

C

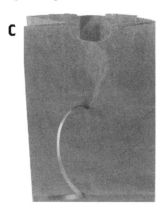

(*Open up the bag and drop the hearts into the bag. Close the bag, grab both ends of the ribbon in one hand, and the bottom of the bag with the other. Pull straight up, tearing the bag. See image d.*)

D

Are you going to let God's Word speak to you today and pierce your heart so it can change your life? (*Reveal the heart pierced and hanging in the middle of the ribbon. See image e.*)

E

ENRICHMENT IDEA

Sword Handling

If you have a small sword, all the better!

While the bag is closed, pierce the sword through at the pencil dot, then open up the bag and keep the bag held up by the sword.

With your free hand, drop the hearts in. Shake the bag using the sword as a handle.

With your free hand, hold the bag at the bottom firmly. Pull thc sword upward to reveal the pierced heart on the sword (image f).

F

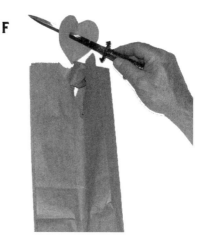

CHAPTER 10
THE CORDS OF SIN

Difficulty Rating: ★★★ Some prop preparation and some method memory.

Effect: A block of wood is tied up with cords, but suddenly breaks free.

Connection: Represents how through Christ's power, we can break free from the bondage of sin.

Scripture: 1 John 1:9

MATERIALS

- Bible with verse reference marked

- 4- to 6-inch length of 4x4 lumber

- power drill with 1- to 2-inch drill bit

- 5- to 6-inch red or pink paper heart

- transparent tape

- 2 4-foot lengths of cord or thin clothesline

- thread the same color as the cord

- scissors

PREPARATION

1. Drill a hole through the center of the lumber.

2. Tape paper heart above the hole.

3. Lay both pieces of the cord together, end to end. Fold each rope in half so the end

of each rope lines up with the other end of the same rope. Bind the centers together by wrapping the thread around both cords a few times and tying a knot. Trim close to the knot (image a). ***Note:*** This same method of secretly tying ropes together is used in "The Lions' Den" (p. 92).

A

4. Thread the block of wood through the ends of the cords (image b).

B

5. Cover the threaded join by centering it inside the block (image c).

C

6. Practice the illusion.

SCRIPT

(Ask two volunteers to help you. Position each volunteer on either side of you. Show the block of wood with the two cords threaded through the middle. Hold on to the block throughout the illusion. You may want to hold the cords in place as you hand them to the volunteers to prevent them from tugging on the cords too soon!)

This block represents your life. All of us want to be free but there is something that robs us of that. That something is sin. Sin is anything we say, think, or do that goes against God's Word. It is also anything we don't say, don't think, or don't do that God's Word says we should do.

(Ask each volunteer to hand you one of the cords on their side. Take these ropes and tie a half knot [images d and e] and hand the ends that end up on the sides back to them to hold along with the other end each has been holding.)

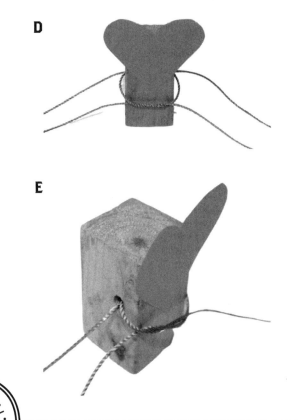

D

E

Sin traps you, just like these cords have trapped the block of wood. It keeps you from living the best possible life—the one that God planned for you. It also robs you of feeling close to God.

Sin can get a really hard hold in your life! There is only one way you can be free from the cords of sin. You need to be forgiven for your sins; you need to be sorry for your sins and ask God to forgive you. *(Read 1 John 1:9.)*

When you ask for forgiveness, God will free you from sin's strong grip. *(Ask volunteers to pull hard on their rope ends. As they do, hold the block tightly and pull up. The thread will snap and the block will come free from the cords.)*

You will be forgiven and free to live the life God has planned for you!

OPTIONAL IDEA

Provide two plastic game rings or plastic bangle bracelets. After tying the knot, ask each volunteer to thread the rings through the cords. When the cords are pulled and the block falls free, the rings will remain on the ropes.

ALTERNATE IDEAS

- Instead of using a paper heart, paint a heart on the wooden block or glue a wooden heart to the block. Drill the hole right through the heart.

- Paint each side of the block one of the colors from Wordless (p. 11) or Jelly-Bean Gospel (p. 14). Use the scripts from those illusions to explain the meanings of the colors.

CHAPTER 11

Cut AND Restored Balloon

Difficulty Rating: ★★★★ Sleight of hand moves needed.

Effect: A balloon is cut in half, but remains filled with air.

Connection: Demonstrates that though we may be broken because of our sin, God can renew our strength.

Scripture: Psalm 23

MATERIALS

- Bible with verse reference marked

- 2 balloons of the same color

- scissors

- box or other location to dispose of scissors and balloon piece

PREPARATION

1. Roll and push one of the balloons inside itself until the bulk of the balloon is inside of the neck (image a).

A

2. Cut the neck off the second balloon (image b).

B

3. Insert the balloons together so that it now appears to be a normal balloon (image c). Hold your fingers at the join, so that no one sees it.

C

4. Practice the illusion.

PRACTICE TIP

Do this in front of a mirror. Watch your hands to ensure you are concealing the loose pieces when needed and that no balloon part is peeking out and destroying the illusion.

SCRIPT

(*Show the assembled balloon.*) Pretend this balloon is like us. We were created to be whole, complete, but then we sinned and that sin hurt us and our relationship with God.

Cutting this balloon represents how broken we are because of sin. (*Pretend to cut the neck off the balloon. Rub the edge of the scissor against the balloon as you move the scissors down and close them. See image d. Put the scissors down and hold up the two separate pieces.*)

D

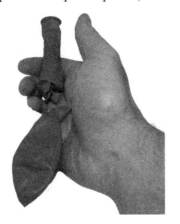

But because of his great love, God can make us whole again. (*Put the pieces in your hands and rub them together. Close one hand to hold the balloon packed into the balloon's neck. Close the other hand to hold the cut balloon.*)

Psalm 23 says the Lord is our shepherd and that he will renew our strength. (*Use the hand with the cut balloon to pull the neck of the good balloon out of your hand a bit. See image e.*)

E

LEFT HAND
WOULD BE CLOSED
IN PERFORMANCE

Jesus died on the cross and rose again. (*Using the hand with the cut balloon, pick up the scissors. Open the scissors to look like a cross. See image f.*)

F

Jesus did this so that we can be forgiven of the sin that makes us broken. (*Wave scissors over the balloon like a magic wand. Put the scissors away in a box or otherwise out of sight and secretly drop the loose piece of cut balloon out of sight.*)

When we accept that forgiveness, God makes us whole. (*Blow into the balloon, and then hold it up.*) Even better than we were before!

Optional: You may want to tie a knot in the balloon and use a permanent marker to draw a cross or heart on the balloon to display for the rest of the lesson.

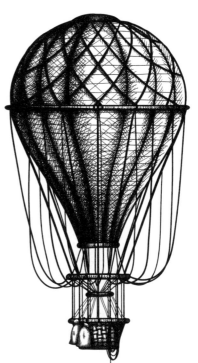

CHAPTER 12

THE RIGHT CHOICE

Difficulty Rating: ★ Print the directions on a card to follow so you can focus on ensuring the kids put their fingers where they are supposed to so it works.

Effect: Twelve squares with choices are shown. A volunteer makes choices and inevitably arrive at Jesus.

Connection: Introduces the idea of seeking God's kingdom first whenever faced with choices.

Scripture: Matthew 6:33.

Additional Scripture: Joshua 24:15, Psalm 25:12, 1 John 2:3–4, or John 15:14.

MATERIALS

• Bible with Scripture references marked

• grid on large sheet of paper

PREPARATION

1. Print the grid (image a) on large sheet of paper. You can change the words on the grid to whatever fits best with your theme.

2. Practice the illusion.

PLAYING WITH FRIENDS	COMPUTER TIME	BOY OR GIRLFRIEND	MONEY
SPORTS	MUSIC	NEW CLOTHES	JESUS
MOVIES	BOOKS	SLEEP	HOMEWORK

USAGE TIP

Use this as an opening activity to introduce your Bible story. All you need is a story that talks about making choices. You can use any words you choose in the other squares, but make sure Jesus stays in the same spot as shown in the grid. Emphasize to the kids that this week's lesson will have a specific choice to make and that no matter the circumstances, following Jesus is always the best choice we can make.

SCRIPT

(*Choose a volunteer or two. Demonstrate what a diagonal move looks like and remind audience which directions are left and right.*)

(*To volunteer.*) Your job is very simple. Just do everything I say! Let's begin. Put a finger on ANY dark square. (*Pause for volunteer to respond.*)

Step one: Move left or right to the nearest light square. What word is in that square? (*Pause for volunteer to respond.*)

Step two: Move up or down to the nearest dark square. What word is in that square? (*Pause for volunteer to respond.*)

Step three: Move diagonally to the nearest light square. What word is in that square? (*Pause for volunteer to respond.*)

Step four: Move left or right to nearest dark square. What word is in that square? (*Pause for volunteer to respond.*)

What word is in that square? Jesus! (*If time allows, repeat with one or more other volunteers.*)

No matter where you start or the direction your week has taken whether it was easy, hard, normal or boring, the right choices should always bring us back to Jesus and what he wants us to do. Matthew 6:33 says seek FIRST the kingdom of God. Doing that will help you then make the next choice and the choice after that and the choice after that!

To apply this story to your life, listen with your ears and heart to this week's Bible story. See what choice Jesus wants YOU to make.

ALTERNATE IDEAS

Instead of drawing the grid on a large sheet of paper, draw it on a white board.

CHAPTER 13

TEMPTATION TAKES HOLD

Difficulty Rating: ★★★✦

Sleight of hand moves needed.

Effect: A glass bottle inexplicably hangs from a rope.

Connection: Shows how temptation can take hold of our lives and hurt us.

Scripture: Matthew 4; James 1:13–15

MATERIALS

- Bible with Scripture references marked

- dark-colored glass bottle

- rope narrow enough to fit in the neck of the bottle, approximately 1.5 feet long

- small rubber ball that fits in the neck of the bottle*

Note: If you can't find a premade ball of the right size, you can make one by carving a cork or rolling up masking tape.

PREPARATION

Practice the illusion.

Optional

Depending on the transparency of the bottle you use, you may need to print and attach a "label" to conceal what's going on inside the bottle (image a).

A

A CLEAR BOTTLE IS USED FOR ILLUSTRATIVE PURPOSES.

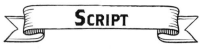

SCRIPT

(*Show an empty bottle. Hold the bottle with your thumb and first finger and conceal the ball in that same hand by curling your other three fingers around the ball.*) This bottle represents temptations—things that cause you to consider sinning, or doing wrong actions. There are lots of different things we can be tempted to do: disobey a parent or teacher, gossip about someone, use angry words to hurt someone, and so on.

The thing is, in the beginning, these temptations seem like they won't do much harm. But if we allow them into our life, they can get ahold of us and grow more powerful and destructive. (*Hand the bottle to a volunteer to examine as you read James 1:13–15 aloud.*)

(*Using the hand concealing the ball, take the opening of the bottle with your thumb and first finger and hold the bottle upside down. See image b. Carefully push the ball into the neck of the bottle as you do, hand the rope to the volunteer to examine.*) Now examine this rope. Anything weird about the rope? Are you sure? Look it over well. (*The audience will look at the rope and the person holding it, giving you enough time to secretly get the ball in the neck of the bottle.*)

B
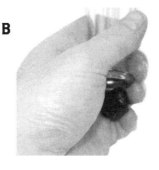

(*Take the rope back while holding the bottle by the neck with your thumb and first fingers. Hold bottle parallel to the floor with the neck towards the palm of your hand. This position helps ensure the ball doesn't roll to the bottom of the bottle but stays closer to the neck where it will be concealed. Hold up the rope.*) This rope represents you. (*Stick an end of the rope into the bottle. Image c.*)

C

Let's review: What does the bottle represent? (*Audience responds.*) What does the rope represent? (*Audience responds.*) Well, now that we've got the rope inserted in the bottle, let's see what happens when you get involved in sin. (*With the rope in the bottle, turn the bottle upside down and let the ball "grab" onto the rope and the neck of the bottle. Pull lightly on the rope to secure the ball and rope in place. Turn the bottle neck up, while maintaining pressure on the rope and bottle. Hold onto the free end of the rope. Let go of the bottle and it will hang in the air illustrating temptation taking hold.*)

Being tempted isn't a sin. In Matthew 4, we learn that Jesus was tempted, and Jesus never sinned. If we give in to temptation and choose it, it takes hold of us and we sin. (*Gently swing the bottle to show the rope has a firm hold.*)

The good news is that we don't have to let sin have that hold on our life. When we sin, we can ask for forgiveness. The power of Jesus then frees us from sin's hold. (*Hold the bottle and loosen the hold on the rope letting the ball go loose in the bottle, but don't let it roll into view. Pull the rope out and hand it to someone to look at. While doing that turn the neck of the bottle to your hand and let the ball secretly roll into your hand. Hand the bottle out to be examined and casually put the ball in your pocket.*)

CHAPTER 14

FOLLOW THE STAR

Difficulty Rating: ★ Practice well so that you get the placement right. Otherwise the effect won't be as smooth.

Effect: Bent toothpicks pull together to make a star.

Connection: Ties in to the Bethlehem star that shone when Jesus was born. Could also be used to talk about creation and how God made the stars, or any verse that talks about stars.

Scripture: Matthew 2:1–12

Note: This illusion is best performed on a table with children gathered around it. The nature of the illusion makes it one kids can do as well, so make sure you have plenty of toothpicks.

MATERIALS

- Bible with verse reference marked

- toothpicks, 5 for each child

- drinking straw

- cup of water

PREPARATION

Remember: "Knowledge is of no value unless you put it into ***practice***." —Anton Chekhov

SCRIPT

At Christmas, the shepherds and wise men followed a star. God was showing people that following is key. We are to follow Jesus, the baby under the star that grew up to be the Savior.

(Have each child bend the toothpicks. Toothpicks should not fully break, but still be connected by some wood fibers. See image a.)

A

(Angle the toothpicks against each other in a tight star burst shape. See image b.)

B

(Draw some water into the straw. Add a couple drops of water in the middle of the toothpicks and the ends of the toothpicks will move out and join, making a star shape. See image c.)

C

(After performing the illusion, work with children as they attempt to replicate it.)

CHAPTER 15

TOMB IS EMPTY

Difficulty Rating: ★★✦ Craft preparation and one small secret move.

Effect: A picture of Jesus is folded into some papers. When the papers are opened again, the picture is gone.

Connection: The papers represent the tomb in which Jesus' body was laid.

Scripture: John 20

MATERIALS

- Bible with verse reference marked

- 8.5x11-inch sheets of colored paper:

    o 1 sheet of yellow paper

    o 2 sheets of blue paper

    o 2 sheets of pink paper

    o 2 sheets of green paper

- scissors

- ruler

- picture of Jesus

- glue stick

Optional

- sheet of white paper

- marker

PREPARATION

1. Cut the two sheets of blue papers to 9.5x7 inches.

2. Cut the two sheets of pink papers to 8x6.25 inches.

3. Cut the two sheets of green papers to 6.5x4.5 inches.

Note: Sheet of yellow paper remains uncut.

4. Fold the green papers. Place them on table so that the papers are taller, rather than wider. Fold the top down and the bottom up so that they meet in the middle. Fold the right and left sides in to center, making sure the right side folds are smaller than the left side.

5. Place each folded green paper to the right of the center of a pink sheet (image a). Fold the top and bottoms of the pink sheets to meet over the folded green paper. Fold the right and left sides over. Again, the right-side fold should be smaller than the left side or center section.

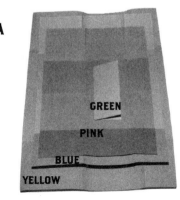

A

GREEN

PINK

BLUE

YELLOW

6. Repeat folding, placing the pink packet of papers on the blue sheets. You should now have two folded blue packets of papers.

7. Repeat folding, placing one of the blue packets on the yellow sheet (image b).

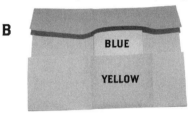

8. Open yellow sheet to remove the blue packet. Open the blue paper and remove the pink packet inside (image c). Set aside. Flip the blue paper upside down.

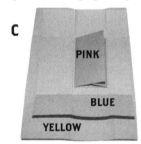

9. Glue the other folded blue packet of papers to the center back of the blue sheet (images d and e). Set aside to dry.

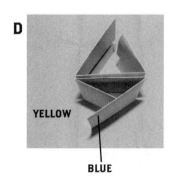
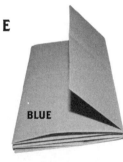

10. When dry, place prepared blue sheet with secret packet on the yellow sheet of paper—packet side down.

11. Place the remaining pink packet of papers in the center of the blue paper and fold up (image f).

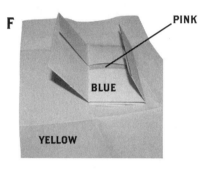

12. Place the blue "double packet" on the yellow sheet (image g) and fold up (image h).

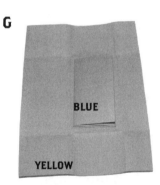

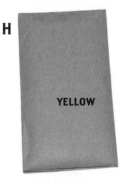

13. Practice the illusion.

Tip: When holding the blue packet keep it angled down so the kids don't see the other packet under it.

Today we're talking about a very sad story. But it's a very important story. In fact, I think it's the most important story of all. This is who the story is about. (*Hold up picture of Jesus. As you say the following, take the folded yellow packet of papers out and begin unfolding. Place each paper on top of the one before, being careful to keep the hidden blue packet away from the audience's view. See image i.*)

I

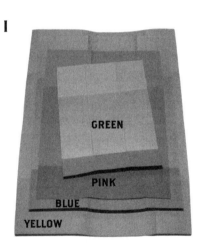

GREEN

PINK

BLUE

YELLOW

You probably have heard a lot about Jesus. Jesus is God's one and only Son. And he came to Earth, taught people about God's great love, and helped hurt people. But even though Jesus did all these good things, there were people who didn't like Jesus. In fact, these people were very angry with Jesus and wanted to stop him. So they told lies and got Jesus arrested, even though he hadn't done anything wrong. Jesus was hurt. In fact, Jesus was killed. (*Fold up and place the picture of Jesus in the center of the green paper.*)

These papers represent the tomb where Jesus' body was laid. A huge rock was rolled in front and guards were posted outside the tomb to ensure nothing could happen to the body.

(*As you speak, fold the papers up, keeping each one flat on the table, on top of the other papers. First fold up the green, then the pink, and then the blue, being careful not to expose the hidden packet. Once the blue packet is folded, pick it up, and as you speak, use it to gesture towards the audience. Then, without looking down at it, casually turn it over and put it on the yellow paper and fold it up.*) But what the angry people didn't know is that all of this was part of God's good plan. Despite their attempts, there was no force on Earth that could stop God's plan. Nothing would stop the miracle that was about to happen!

Three days after his death, some of Jesus friends came to the tomb. They were met with an amazing surprise! The Bible tells us in John 20 that the HUGE rock was rolled away from the tomb's opening. But even more surprisingly . . . (*Unfold the papers to show the Jesus picture is not there.*) The tomb was empty! Jesus was not there. Jesus is alive!

Place a folded up paper with the words, "The tomb was empty" in the green packet that ends up in the hidden blue packet. When you open up the packets the kids will think it is still the Jesus picture, until your final reveal!

Difficulty Rating: ★★★ There is some challenge in remembering the right way to "shuffle" and arrange the deck.

Effect: The commandment tablets are mixed up and eliminated and the last halves end up matching. As a kicker the rest are turned over and they match!

Connection: This illusion is played like a game with a surprise ending. The rules of the game reinforce the need for rules, and the papers depict the Ten Commandments.

Scripture: Exodus 20

MATERIALS

- Bible with verse reference marked

- printable stone tablets

- 5 different colors of paper

- glue stick

- white card stock

- scissors

- marker

- sheet of white paper

PREPARATION

1. Search online for an image of stone tablets or copy the one on page 44. Print the tablets onto each of the five different colors of papers.

2. Glue the colored tablets onto separate sheets of white card stock.

3. Cut each page in half horizontally.

4. Use marker to print "Last Two Cards Match" on the white sheet of paper.

5. Place the tablet TOPS on a table in a row. Place the BOTTOMS in a row beneath the TOPS. Make sure the colors align, top to bottom (image a).

A

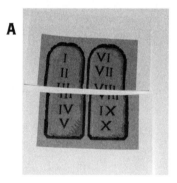

6. Practice the illusion.

SCRIPT

Today we're going to talk about the Ten Commandments. Put your hands on your head if you've heard of them before. (*Audience responds.*) Exodus 20 in the Bible tells us about when God told Moses these ten rules for living the best life possible. I'm sure you all have heard about rules before! Well, these rules were written by God on large stone tablets. (*Show the TOPS and BOTTOMS you prepared.*)

Well, rules are important to games, and we're going to play a game with our colored commandment cards. But I'm going to let my volunteer chose some of the rules. Who would like to be my volunteer? (*As you select a volunteer and they make their way to you, collect the TOPS from the left to the right placing each card ON TOP the one previously picked up. Place the pile facedown on the table.*)

(*Next, collect the BOTTOMS from right to left placing each card on top of the one previously picked up. Place the pile facedown on the table. See image b. This image shows the order of each pile. In performance, they remain facedown!*)

B

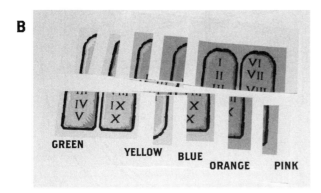

GREEN YELLOW BLUE ORANGE PINK

(*Ask volunteer to choose either top or bottom pile and hold it facedown in their hand. It doesn't matter which pile they choose. Hold the remaining pile facedown in your hand.*)

The rules are this: We are going to shuffle cards according to a prediction I have made and then eliminate our cards until we each are left with ONE card. My prediction is (*Hold up prediction paper so audience can read.*) that the last two cards, the last one of mine and that last one from (volunteer), will match!

We will use the letters in my prediction to guide our shuffling. Our first shuffle is based on the word *last*, L-A-S-T. For each letter, we will take turns removing the top card from our pile and placing it on the bottom. Then, at the end of the word, we will both toss out the top card. Who do you want to go first? (*Volunteer chooses which player goes first–them or the leader. For L, the first player will move the top card to the bottom of the pile. On A, the other player moves the top card to the bottom of the pile. Repeat, alternating players for S and T.*)

(*When the word is spelled, both players remove their top card. Put these two cards together and place them off to the side. Don't show the faces or give these any attention until the end.*)

Now we have the word *two*, T-W-O. (*Volunteer chooses who will go first and action is repeated as with the first word. Place the discarded cards together and place in a separate pile. Repeat with the words* cards *and* match.)

(*Players will now each have one card remaining. Turn cards over to show that they match and that your prediction was correct.*)

(*Reveal the pairs of cards in the discarded piles, and show that THEY match also!*)

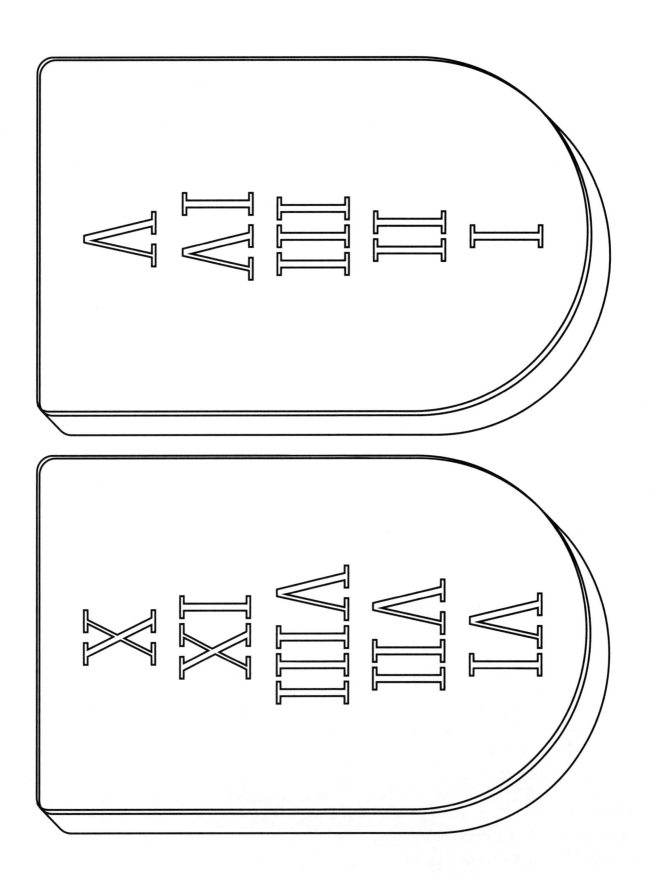

CHAPTER 17

LIFE IN JESUS

Difficulty Rating: ★ You may crack a few eggs preparing it. Plan to eat omelets or bake after completing your preparation.

Effect: Two eggs are cracked open. One has the usual yolk and white of an egg. The other is empty.

Connection: Illustrates how full and rich life is when centered on Jesus, and how empty a life centered on the world is.

Scripture: Acts 14:15, John 10:10.

Additional Scripture:
John 1:3–4 and Ephesians 4.

MATERIALS

- Bible with Scripture references marked

- 2 (or more) eggs

- small nail

- bowl

- permanent marker

PREPARATION

1. Take an egg and poke a small hole in the top (images a and b).

    A
    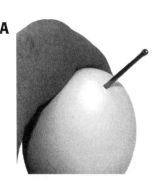

    B

2. At the bottom of the egg, poke a slightly larger hole (image c).

    C
    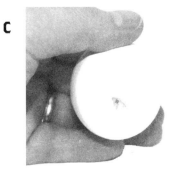

3. Over a bowl, blow hard into the egg's small hole. The contents of the egg will squish out the bigger hole and land (hopefully) in the bowl.

4. Wash out the egg and set aside to dry.

5. When egg is dry, use a permanent marker to print the word *World* on it.

6. Print *Jesus* on a second, normal egg.

7. Practice the illusion.

SCRIPT

We have a choice each day to pursue Jesus (*Hold up "Jesus" egg.*) or the things of the world (*Hold up "World" egg.*).

One choice gives us life. In John 10:10, the Bible tells us Jesus said, "My purpose is to give [my followers] a rich and satisfying life." (*Crack the "Jesus" egg open and pour contents into a bowl, showing the yolk representing life. Share an age-appropriate example of a time that Jesus made your life fuller.*)

The other choice is to pursue the things of the world. (*Hold up "World" egg. Share some common pursuits of the world applicable to your group and share how they ultimately are empty and unsatisfying.*)

(*Crack the "World" egg open and show it is empty.*) Just like this egg, pursuing the things of the world makes our life empty. In Acts 14:5, we hear the words of the apostles Paul and Barnabas, "We have come to bring you the Good News that you should turn from these worthless things and turn to the living God, who made heaven and earth, the sea, and everything in them."

CHAPTER 18

STRENGTH WHEN HURT

Difficulty Rating: ★

Effect: A resealable plastic bag of water is pierced with pencils, but no water leaks out.

Connection: Illustrates the biblical truth that no matter how many difficulties may pierce our lives, the Holy Spirit remains in us and will hold us together.

Scripture: Job, Psalm 23:4, Isaiah 53:5, John 14:26–27, 2 Corinthians 1:3–5

MATERIALS

- Bible with Scripture references marked

- sharp pencils

- resealable plastic sandwich bag

- water

- shallow tray or plastic bin

Optional:

- tags, one for each pencil

- marker

- transparent tape

PREPARATION

1. Fill resealable plastic sandwich bag two-thirds full with water.

2. Practice the illusion.

Optional

For each pencil, print the word "Hurt" on a tag and tape it to the pencil.

PRACTICE TIP

- Whatever you do, don't pull the pencil back out once you've pierced the bag!

- Sharp pencils help the poking happen smoothly.

- Push the pencils through as straight as possible.

- Having a few drops spill out is normal. The drips should stop quickly.

- Have a couple of bags prepared in case you have an issue the first time.

- Hold the plastic bags over the shallow tray or plastic bin.

We live in a sin-filled world where there is hurt and pain everywhere. We can be living the right way, doing the right things, and still end up hurt. Job is just one example from the Bible of someone this happened to. (*Expand on Job's story, as time permits.*)

God doesn't promise that we will go through life and never be hurt. But he does promise that he will be with us. Psalm 23:4 says, "Even when I walk through the darkest valley, I will not be afraid, for you are close beside me. Your rod and your staff protect and comfort me." Knowing this can give us strength when hurts come at us.

These pencils represent different hurts. (*Hold up pencils.*)

The bag represents us (*Hold up water-filled bag.*), and the water represents God's Holy Spirit in us. In John 14:26–27, Jesus promises to send us the Holy Spirit to be with us, to comfort us, and to guide us to live the very best life—the life God has planned for us.

So when trouble and hurts come our way . . . (*Pierce the bag through both sides with the pencils. Keep the pencils in the bag. No water will spill out. See image below*)

God gives us the strength to handle what will come. Aren't you thankful for that? God's Spirit is a healer and comforter who can help us when hurtful things happen to us.

Option 1: Building off 2 Corinthians 1:3–5, you can lead into a strong application. Challenge kids to reach out and comfort those around them who need support. Remind children that God is with them and will help them to help others.

Option 2: Put red food coloring in the water and use it to symbolize the blood Jesus shed when he was pierced for our transgressions (Isaiah 53:5). Remind children that Jesus willingly allowed himself to be hurt and that the whole time, he was in control. His blood was only shed because Jesus allowed it, and he allowed it so that we could be forgiven for our sin. At that point, pull the pencils out and let the red water pour out into the tray or bin.

CHAPTER 19
WORD OF GOD ENDURES

Difficulty Rating: ★★★ You have to secretly conceal something in your hand, and you have to act surprised when the "trick goes wrong."

Effect: A strip of paper with the word BIBLE written on it is torn up, unfolded, and restored. In doing that a bundle of paper drops. It appears that the trick backfired. You then open up the dropped bundle and reveal a picture of the Bible.

Connection: Illustrates that God's Word never fails and that it will stand firm forever. Useful for introducing any Bible story or verse.

Scripture: Isaiah 40:8

MATERIALS

- Bible with verse reference marked

- Picture of a Bible

- 2 strips of paper, approximately 3x8 inches in size

- marker

- glue stick

PREPARATION

1. Print the word *BIBLE* on each strip of paper.

2. Take one of the BIBLE strips and accordion-fold it.

3. On the other BIBLE strip, apply some glue on the back of the strip behind the first *B*.

4. Stick that strip to the back of the accordion-folded Bible strip behind the first *B* (image a).

5. Fold the Bible picture into a small packet, about the same size as the accordion-folded paper strip.

6. Practice the illusion.

Optional

Instead of using a marker, use a word-processing application on your computer and a printer to print the word *BIBLE* twice on a sheet of paper. Cut the strips from the paper and continue as described above.

SCRIPT

(Secretly hold the folded Bible picture in your right hand. Hold the Bible strip up, holding on either end with each hand.) The Bible is God's words for us. It is a book like no other. In Isaiah 40:8, the Bible tells us that "The grass withers and the flowers fade, but the word of our God stands forever."

The Bible has survived mankind's attempts to discredit it *(Tear the B off. Place it BEHIND the rest of the word.)*

To keep it away from people *(Rip the I off. Place it behind the first B.)*

To say it is outdated *(Rip the second B off. Place it behind the I.)*

And to claim that it is wrong. *(Rip the L off. Place it behind the second B. Then place the E behind the L.)*

(Fold the torn pieces together in a bundle so they will stay together.)

Tip: Ensure the torn edges are folded smaller than the width of the strip so that when it is opened no telltale pieces show (image b).

B

(Casually turn the packet over left to right. You now have the torn pieces folded and facing you. The accordion-folded strip is facing the audience.)

God's Word endures, it lasts forever!

(As you "spring open" the accordion-folded paper, drop the folded Bible picture on the ground. See image c. Act embarrassed. Put aside the Bible word strip and torn pieces.)

C

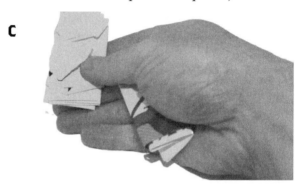

(Show that your hands are empty and then pick up the packet on the ground. Open it up to reveal the picture of the Bible.)

Like I said, God's Word endures forever!

BIBLE

BIBLE

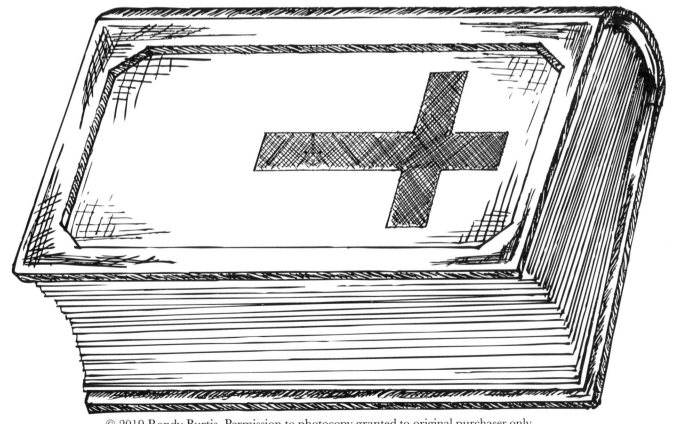

Instant Bible Lessons: *Gospel Illusions: Object Lessons You Can Do!*

CHAPTER 20

HELPING HAND

Difficulty Rating: ★★★ Practice "The Secret Move" and make sure the ropes aren't too tight or too loose on volunteers' wrists.

Effect: Two people's hands are roped up and linked. They need help from you to get free.

Connection: Represents our inability to solve sin problems without help provided by God.

Scripture: Galatians 5:1, Colossians 3:13

MATERIALS

- Bible with Scripture references marked

- 2 lengths of soft rope

- towel

PREPARATION

1. Use marker to print the word *forgiveness* written on a sheet of paper. Pin paper onto towel.

2. Practice the illusion.

SCRIPT

There are sins we do that only affect us and our relationship with God. There are other sins that also affect others! When we sin against someone or they sin against us, that sin entangles us and traps us. We need a helping hand to get it untangled.

(Tie a rope around the wrists of the first volunteer. Tie the second rope around one of the second person's wrists, then drape rope over the first volunteer's rope, pick it up again, and tie the end to the second person's other wrist. See image a.)

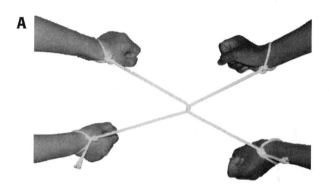

Who is someone who is ALWAYS there to help us—no matter where we go, no matter what we're doing? (Jesus). Jesus has paved a way for us to ask forgiveness for ourselves and to give forgiveness to others. In Colossians 3:13, the Bible says we are to "Make allowance for each other's faults, and forgive anyone who offends you. Remember, the Lord forgave you, so you must forgive others."

(Drape towel over the hands and rope, do The Secret Move. See below.)

God will help us be free and forgiven. Galatians 5:1 says, "Christ has truly set us free!" Have the volunteers step apart, freed. Display the towel with the word "forgiveness" on it prominently.

THE SECRET MOVE

Once both volunteers' wrists are tied with the ropes linked (image b), cover wrists with the towel. The images here are shown without the towel for illustrative purposes.

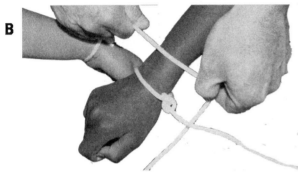

Lift one rope over the top of one of the other kid's wrists (image c).

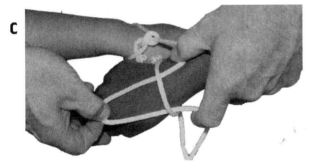

Push that rope UNDER the wrist and toward the kid's fingers (image d).

Push that rope over their fingers then pull it out of the bottom of their wrist and they will be unlinked! Practice this move so you are just under the cover two or three seconds.

PRACTICE TIPS

- If you don't have a couple of kids at home on whom to inflict your practice (like I do!), use chairs instead. Place two chairs on their side. Cut slits in tennis balls and put balls on the end of the top two legs of each chair. The balls will be like closed fists and the legs of the chairs like arms. You can then tie the ropes as instructed and practice the move—first without the towel and then with the towel until you get the action down smooth.

- A bigger towel is recommended so it doesn't drop off with the movement prematurely.

CHAPTER 21

GOD FORGIVES

Difficulty Rating: ★☆ Requires dexterity and practice.

Effect: A rope with a knot is lowered into a cylinder. When the rope is lifted out of the cylinder, the knot is gone.

Connection: The knot represents sin. The cylinder represents God's forgiveness. The seeming disappearance of the knot represents how God removes sin from our lives.

Scripture: Matthew 6:14, Ephesians 4:31–32, Psalm 103:12

MATERIALS

- Bible with Scripture references marked

- marker

- sheet of paper

- tape

- pool noodle

- scissors

- 24- to 30-inch length of soft, thin rope

PREPARATION

1. In large letters, use marker to print the words *God forgives* on the sheet of paper. Tape the paper to the front of the cylinder.

2. Cut pool noodle into a cylinder approximately 6 to 8 inches long. On the back of the cylinder, cut out a hole for your thumb to fit in (image a).

A

3. With the rope, tie a loose knot (image b). Make sure knot is loose enough that you can slide your thumb in the middle of the knot (image c).

B

C

IN ORDER TO UNKNOT PROPERLY, THE KNOT NEEDS TO MAINTAIN THIS ORIENTATION WHEN YOUR THUMB IS PLACED IN IT. THE END HELD BY FINGERS IN THE IMAGE SHOULD BE AT THE BOTTOM OF THE CONTAINER.

4. Practice the illusion.

Note: Once you've practiced the illusion, you may find using your index finger in the knot feels more comfortable than using your thumb. Use whichever feels best.

SCRIPT

(*Hold up rope.*) This rope represents us and the knot represents sin we may have in our lives. When there is sin in our lives, it gets in the way. Things just aren't right. And the one thing we'd like to do is get rid of it!

Ephesians 4:31–32 says, "Get rid of all bitterness, rage, anger, harsh words, and slander, as well as all types of evil behavior. Instead, be kind to each other, tenderhearted, forgiving one another, just as God through Christ has forgiven you." Not only SHOULD we forgive others, but Matthew 6:14 promises, "If you forgive those who sin against you, your heavenly Father will forgive you." What an incredible promise!

(*Hold up cylinder.*) This cylinder represents God's desire to forgive us. (*Lower rope into the tube. Let the knot go out the bottom of the cylinder and then bring it back up to the middle of the cylinder. When the loose knot lines up with the secret hole in the back of the cylinder, secretly poke your thumb through the hole and into the center of the knot. See image d.*)

D

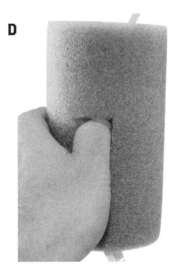

(As you then raise the rope back up the knot will undo around your thumb. See image e. As the rope is removed from the cylinder, the "sin" is gone.) When we ask God to forgive our sins, he will! God can forgive ANY sin, no matter how big or small. Psalm 103:12 tells us that "[God] has removed our sins as far from us as the east is from the west." You can't get farther than that!

E

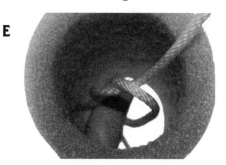

MAKE SURE THE KIDS CAN'T SEE YOU PUT YOUR FINGER IN THE HOLE!

Any time you have someone helping in a hands-on way, you're adding layers of engagement to the presentation and making it that much more memorable for all.

If you are feeling bold, you can have a kid lower the rope in and pull it back out of the cylinder.

- Show volunteer the speed at which you want them to move the rope.

- Tie the knot, lower it in the cylinder, with your other hand covering the hole on the back. Just make sure you keep the top of the container higher than their eye level.

- Give volunteer the knotted rope.

- Place one hand flat on the front of the container and the other at the back with your index finger close to the secret hole. If you angle the hole closer to you, you will conceal when you put your finger in and your front arm will block any telltale signs the rest of the group might see.

- Instruct the volunteer to lower the rope through the cylinder so that the knot shows under the bottom.

- Have the volunteer slowly raise the rope.

- Slide your index finger in the knot so that the rope can be pulled from the cylinder knot-free.

CHAPTER 22
KNOWN BY GOD

Difficulty Rating: ★

Effect: Colored pom-poms are put in a bag. Blindly reach into the bag and choose a pom-pom, closing your hand around the pom-pom and pulling your hand from the bag. Before opening your hand, correctly guess the color. Can be repeated several times.

Connection: The illusionist's apparently amazing knowledge of the pom-pom colors parallels God's amazing knowledge of us.

Scripture: Luke 12:7, 1 Peter 5:7

MATERIALS

- Bible with Scripture references marked

- brown paper lunch bag

- colored craft pom-poms

- clear plastic wrap

- transparent tape

PREPARATION

1. Cut a hole in the back of the bag, at the bottom where the bag creases when folded flat.

2. Cover the hole with clear wrap, taping wrap in place. Fold up the bag so the window is concealed. See image a, which shows pom-poms inside the bag so you can see the window.

A

3. Practice the illusion.

Note: You can casually show the folded bag, both sides, even with the window in it as long as you don't make the window too big and keep the bag folded flat.

SCRIPT

(*Hold up the different colored pom-poms.*) Here I have many different colors of pom-poms. (*Hold up folded bag.*) I will now place the pom-poms in this bag. (*Open the bag up with the secret window towards you and dump the balls in.*) I will now shake it up! (*Shake bag.*)

I will now reach into the bag and before opening my hand, tell you the color of the pom-pom.

Do you think I can do it? (*Reach in and grab a pom-pom. Glimpse through the window to see the color of the pom-pom, and then conceal it in your hand.*)

Ah! This feels like a good pom-pom. Now, before I pull my hand out of the bag I will close my eyes, (*Close eyes.*) pull the pom-pom from the bag (*Pull pom-pom from bag.*), and tell you the color. This pom-pom is [RED]! (*Open hand and reveal pom-pom. Open your eyes. Repeat two or three times.*)

Are you impressed that I could know the color of the pom-pom? I know something even MORE impressive. God knows you so well; he knows the number of hairs on your head. Luke 12:7 in the Bible says that "the very hairs on your head are all numbered. So don't be afraid; you are more valuable to God than a whole flock of sparrows."

Today's lesson has an amazing truth from God's heart to yours. God knows everything about you and cares about you. In 1 Peter 5:7, we read, "Give all your worries and cares to God, for he cares about you." God knows you, he knows the type of week you had and the type of week you will have, and what cares and concerns will come your way.

God wants you to carry today's truth close to your heart. Because he knows you, he knows exactly what you will need this week.

ALTERNATE IDEA

Use this to teach a point that God knows our actions and we can't hide our sins from him. Create a list of sins familiar to your kids (lying, disobeying, stealing, etc.). Then perform the illusion, pulling a color, naming it, and assigning it to a sin, and talking about that sin.

It may seem amazing or maybe even a little scary that I can know something that you can't see, something that is hidden in the bag. Sometimes we do sins that we think others don't see. But God sees everything.

SCRIPT

This truth isn't there to scare you, but it can motivate us to stay honest before God. It can help us to not pile up a bunch of sins we THINK no one knows about. God knows. And what's amazing is that he's always ready to forgive us. He loves us anyway!

God wants us to live the best lives possible. God wants to help us grow and walk with integrity. *Integrity* means that our words and actions are the same whether we think we are being seen or not. When we walk with integrity, we aren't trying to hide anything. This is great, because living a fake life can be really exhausting! And a waste of time because God knows it all anyway!

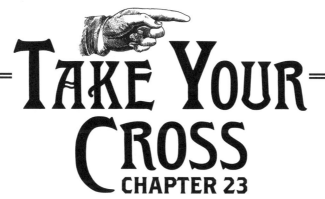

TAKE YOUR CROSS
CHAPTER 23

Difficulty Rating: ★★ Some arts and crafts.

Effect: Two crosses are removed from a puzzle.

Connection: Emphasizes the need for us to take up our cross daily and follow Jesus.

Scripture: Matthew 16:24–26, Jeremiah 29:11

MATERIALS

- Bible with Scripture references marked

- scissors or craft knife

- index card

- curling ribbon or string

- 2 small crosses with key rings or bails

- marker

- stopwatch

PREPARATION

1. Use scissors or craft knife to cut two slits about a half inch apart along the center of the index card (image a).

2. Cut a hole at the bottom of the index card that is slightly larger than the slit above it (image a).

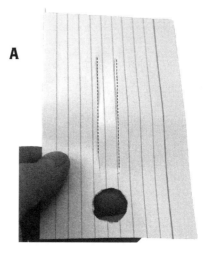

A

3. At the top of the card, print, "Deny yourself." At the bottom, print, "Take up the cross."

4. Cut a length of curling ribbon approximately 12 inches long.

5. Thread the ribbon through the slit in the card and then through the hole at the bottom (see image on next page).

6. Knot a cross to each end of the ribbon (image b).

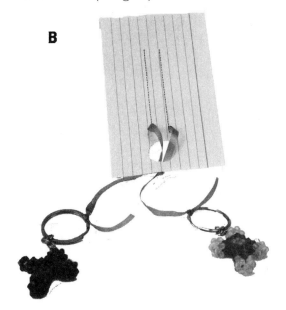

B

7. Practice the illusion.

Optional: Instead of an index card, use a playing card.

Note: You may wish to prepare a couple of extra cross puzzles in case volunteers accidentally tear them while trying to solve the puzzle.

SCRIPT

(*Choose one or more volunteers. Hand each volunteer a cross puzzle.*) The challenge is to remove the crosses from the card without tearing the card or untying the crosses from the ribbon. If you can't get them off in 20 seconds, you have to shout, "I surrender." (*Time volunteers. Encourage audience to count down the last 10 seconds with you.*)

In the book of Matthew, chapter 16, verses 24–26, Jesus spoke to his followers about denying themselves and taking up their cross.

> *Then Jesus said to his disciples, "If any of you wants to be my follower, you must give up your own way, take up your cross, and follow me. If you try to hang on to your life, you will lose it. But if you give up your life for my sake, you will save it. And what do you benefit if you gain the whole world but lose your own soul? Is anything worth more than your soul?"*

When we look at this puzzle, it reminds us that trying to take up the cross is not easy. It is a daily challenge. But if you know the secret, you can do it. The secret is to surrender your plans and allow God to be the one in control.

(*Turn your back to the audience and slide a finger under the strip created by the slits. See image c.*)

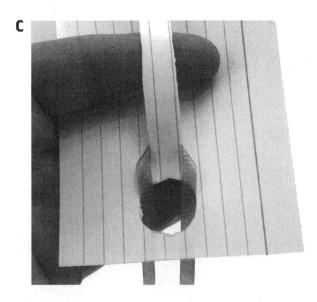

C

(Push the center of the strip through the hole, creating a loop. See image d.)

D

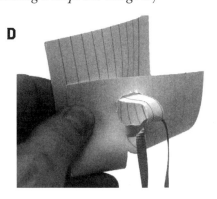

(Pull the ribbon and attached cross through the loop. See image e.)

E

(Straighten the card out, shout "I surrender!" turn around, and show the crosses released.)

When you couldn't do the puzzle and shouted "I surrender", you were denying yourself and taking up your cross, just like Jesus said. Every day we must surrender: surrender our plans, surrender our wishes, and to the extreme, even surrender our lives in order to follow him.

On the surface that can sound harsh and mean, but Jeremiah 29:11 tells us

"'For I know the plans I have for you,' says the LORD. 'They are plans for good and not for disaster, to give you a future and a hope.'"

Although it can be truly hard to surrender, to give up our ways, God has something that is ultimately better for us.

ENRICHMENT IDEA

Turn this into a craft activity and show the kids how to get the crosses removed from the card.

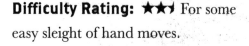

CHAPTER 24
JESUS ENTERS THE LOCKED ROOM

Difficulty Rating: ★★✦ For some easy sleight of hand moves.

Effect: A coin appears to move through the sides of a solid handkerchief.

Connection: Represents how Jesus suddenly appeared in a locked room, as if he'd moved through the walls.

Scripture: John 20:19–21; Revelation 3:20

MATERIALS

- Bible with Scripture references marked

- permanent marker

- largest coin you have

- handkerchief

PREPARATION

1. With permanent marker, draw a cross on the coin.

2. Practice the illusion.

SCRIPT

Jesus did the impossible all the time. Not only was his resurrection from the dead impossible, but he continued to do MORE impossible things after that! One of the amazing, impossible things Jesus did is told in John 20:19–21:

> *That Sunday evening the disciples were meeting behind locked doors because they were afraid of the Jewish leaders. Suddenly, Jesus was standing there among them! "Peace be with you," he said. As he spoke, he showed them the wounds in his hands and his side. They were filled with joy when they saw the Lord! Again he said, "Peace be with you. As the Father has sent me, so I am sending you."*

Jesus did something impossible! He suddenly appeared out of nowhere to his followers—even though they were in a locked room!

(*Hold up coin.*) Here is a coin. I drew a cross on it to represent Jesus. Just like Jesus somehow made his way into a locked room, this coin will make its way through this handkerchief (*Hold up handkerchief.*), without damaging the handkerchief.

(Hold the coin at your fingertips. See image a.)

A

(Cover the coin and your hand with the handkerchief. See image b.)

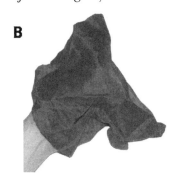

B

(Push a bit of extra handkerchief between your thumb and the coin. See image c.)

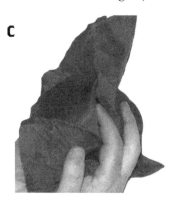

C

(Take the edge of the handkerchief that is farthest from you and bring it over the top and towards you, revealing to the audience that the coin is still there. See image d.)

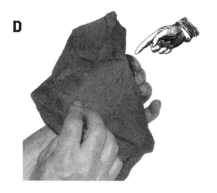

D

(Take BOTH edges of the handkerchief and flip them back over the coin. See image e.)

E

(Performers view: The audience won't see the coin exposed, they will see the shape of a coin in the handkerchief. Fold the edges of the handkerchief over the coin holding it snuggly. See image f.)

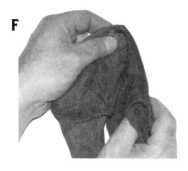

F

(Image g shows what the audience will see.)

G

(Start to twist the handkerchief at the bottom of the coin and it will appear to be pushed through the center of the handkerchief. See image h.)

H

(Take the coin out and open up the handkerchief showing no holes. See image i.)

I

If Jesus could do the impossible and come into a locked room, he could come into a heart that was closed to him. But Jesus is a gentleman. He will not force his way into your life. Revelation 3:20 tells us that Jesus will knock at the door of our heart and we must let him in.

You may know someone for whom it seems impossible for Jesus to get into their life and their heart. But remember: Jesus can do the impossible. Remember our verse earlier that told us Jesus said he is sending us? Our job is to keep our eyes open and pray for others to hear Jesus knocking on their heart and for them to respond by opening the door to Jesus and make the decision to love and follow Jesus. That's when we will see the impossible happen in their life!

CHAPTER 25

TRUST NOT IN MONEY

Difficulty Rating: ★★ You have to conceal a coin in your hand for a short time and remember the paper fold.

★★★ For the Alternate Idea (p. 66) as it requires more tricky moves.

Effect: A coin is trapped in folded paper. It then vanishes.

Connection: Reinforces the biblical truth that we need to trust in God, not money. Also, because God will provide all that we need, we can be generous with others.

Scripture: Luke 12:16–31

Additional Scripture: Luke 16:19–31

- Bible with Scripture references marked

- coin

- square of paper approximately three times the size of the coin

"In theory there is no difference between theory and **practice**. In **practice** there is." —Yogi Berra

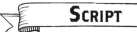

(*Hold up coin.*) How many of you like coins? (*Audience responds. Take the coin and put it on the square of paper. Place it in the center and just a bit lower than the middle. See image a.*)

A

I think everyone likes money. Or at least they like the things money can buy. (*Fold the bottom half up over the coin. Don't fold the paper flush on the top. Fold it a few millimeters lower than the edge. See image b.*)

B

There was a man who was so focused on trying to get as much money as he could. He was putting his trust in money to look after him. (*Crease the bottom fold. While you are doing this, nonchalantly rub the impression of the coin onto the paper.*)

We all need things that money can buy. Things like food, clothing, and shelter. But some of the things we want aren't really things we need. (*Fold the left side back, away from you, repeat with the right side. Don't fold too close to the actual coin. Leave some room for the coin to move. See image c.*)

C

And even when it comes to the things we need? God promises to provide what we need, so is there any reason to think about, worry about, or be stingy with money all the time? (*Audience will respond, "NO!"*)

(*Turn the packet 180 degrees. Squeeze the edges lightly and the coin will secretly drop into your hand. See image d.*)

D

(*Fold the top edge away from you and place it on the table so that the last folded edge is TOWARD you.*)

You are right. Listen to what Jesus tells his disciples. (*Reach for your Bible as you casually put the coin in your pocket. Due to the impression the coin made on the paper, it looks like it is still there. Read Luke 12:16–31 aloud.*)

If we put God first he will provide all we need. Trust in God, not money and things. (*Tear up the paper, revealing that the coin is gone.*)

ALTERNATE IDEA

(*Before doing the illusion, print the word TRUST on an envelope. As you begin to perform the illusion, ask a volunteer to mark the coin with a permanent marker. They can use their initials, draw a happy face, or in any way they want, mark the coin.*)

(*Then, instead of slipping the coin in a pocket, hold it in your hand concealed. See image e. Keep your hand loose and curled and the coin will stay there. In the minds of the audience, the coin is still trapped in the paper on the table.*)

E

(*Retrieve the envelope you prepared and hand it to the volunteer to examine.*) Examine the envelope. Is there anything funny about it? Look in it and on it and under it and in any other way you can. Other than the word *TRUST* being printed on it, it is just an ordinary envelope right? (*Volunteer responds.*) Great! I'm just going to take it back and seal it closed. Should I use my spit or tape? (*As audience is responding, work the coin from your fingers onto the back of the envelope. See image f.*)

F

Well, if you said you wanted tape, I can't find it! So I'm going to use my spit. (*As you respond, casually tuck coin into the envelope. See image g.*)

G

(*Lick and seal envelope. Set aside. See image h.*)

H

(*Continue with reading Luke 12:16–31 and teaching about trusting in Jesus to provide. After you rip up the folded paper and reveal the coin gone, show your hands unmistakably empty. Then pick up the sealed envelope, rip it open, and show the coin concealed inside. Ask volunteer to verify that the coin has the mark they drew on it.*) As we trust God, he will provide money for us in amazing ways!

CHAPTER 26

MULTIPLYING MONEY

Difficulty Rating: ★★★ Some arts and craft preparation to make the special plate.

Effect: Seven coins are counted out on a plate, and then poured into a child's hands. Counted again, the number of coins has grown to ten.

Connection: Illustrates the fact that you can't outgive God. Also could be used in any Bible story that talks about coins, such as the widow who gave all she had (Mark 12:41–44) or the woman who searched for her lost coin (Luke 15:8–10).

Scripture: Luke 6:38, Malachi 3:10

MATERIALS

- Bible with Scripture references marked

- 2 paper plates

- craft knife

- glue

- cardboard strips

- 10 coins of the same value (pennies, nickels, or dimes work well)

PREPARATION

1. Using a craft knife, cut a slot out of the side of one of the paper plates. The slot should be a bit wider and taller than the coins you will use (image a).

A

2. On the bottom of the plate, glue cardboard strips leading from the opening to create a pocket for the coins. Make the strips a bit higher than the height of the coins. Place a strip or two in between and perpendicular to the strips to help secure the second plate (images b and c).

B

C

3. Place a line of glue on the cardboard strips and around the edges of the plate.

4. Place second paper plate on top, covering the secret pocket and slot (image d).

D

5. If you haven't already secured the coins in the pocket, slide three coins into the secret slot. Spread the remaining seven coins out on the top of the plate.

6. Practice the illusion.

SCRIPT

(Select a volunteer. Making sure your hand blocks the secret slot, have the volunteer count out loud the number of coins on the plate. Show the audience that your hands are empty and also have volunteer show that their hands are also empty.)

Luke 6:38 tells us that God says, "Give, and you will receive." I am going to give you these seven coins. Cup your hands so that I can pour them in. I don't want to touch them. Then close your hands around them so I can't get to them.

(Move the plate so that the slot is towards the volunteer. Pour the seven coins into their hands and let the other three coins slide in also. The volunteer won't notice. Put the plate aside.)

God loves to provide. When we are faithful and obey him, he will take what we give and use it, multiply it, and grow it. In Malachi 3:10, God promises his people that if they will bring in their tithes, he will "open the windows of heaven for you. I will pour out a blessing so great you won't have enough room to take it in! Try it! Put me to the test!"

(Mime taking a coin out of the air and toss it towards volunteer's hands. Repeat two more times.)

You had seven coins I gave you three more . . . Did you see it? So how many coins do you have? Seven plus three equals ten.

(Volunteer counts out the ten coins on the plate, again keeping your hand covering the secret slot.)

We don't always see how God will use what we give, but we can trust him that he will use it in the very best way possible.

CHAPTER 27

FLIP FLOP

Difficulty Rating: ★★★↙ You have to watch the angle of your hand and do the secret move smoothly.

Effect: A rubber band jumps back and forth between fingers.

Connection: Illustrates that we cannot flip back and forth between serving two masters.

Scripture: Matthew 6:24, 1 John 2:15–17

MATERIALS

- Bible with Scripture references marked

- rubber band

PREPARATION

"Practice puts brains in your muscles." —Sam Snead

SCRIPT

Matthew 6:24 tells us, "No one can serve two masters. For you will hate one and love the other; you will be devoted to one and despise the other." God wants to be our master. But too many Christians are flippy floppy. On Sunday they say that God is their master and that they are on God's side.

(Point to rubber band over the middle and pointer fingers.)

Then they leave church and don't do what they know they should. They flip over and live in the world, following its lead—the opposite of God's ways.

(Do The Secret Move described on the next page. Open your hand to show rubber band flipped over the pinky and ring fingers.)

1 John 2: 15–17 warns us,

> *Do not love this world nor the things it offers you, for when you love the world, you do not have the love of the Father in you. For the world offers only a craving for physical pleasure, a craving for everything we see, and pride in our achievements and possessions. These are not from the Father, but are from this world. And this world is fading away, along with everything that people crave. But anyone who does what pleases God will live forever.*

God will help us choose his side and stay there. All we have to do is ask for his help.

(Do The Secret Move again. Open your hand to show rubber band flipped over the first and second fingers again.)

THE SECRET MOVE

Begin with the rubber band over the first two fingers (image a).

A

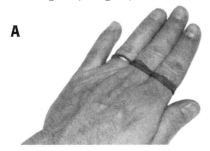

Close your hand into a fist (image b). Use your other hand to "adjust" the rubbing band, making sure it is down as far as it could be on your fingers.

B

Images c and d are from your perspective. When you "adjust" the band, you will pull the elastic down (image c) and place all four fingers into it (image d). This move takes less than a second.

C

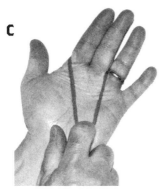

D

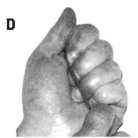

Open your hand (image e). The elastic has jumped fingers!

E

Image f is a stop-action shot of what happens as the hand is opened.

F

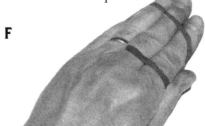

PERFORMANCE TIP

As with anything you wish to do well, practice is the key. Use a mirror to help you position your hand properly so that you know the audience will see what they are supposed to see, and not see what they aren't supposed to see.

A key is to take some time adjusting and fiddling with the elastic on the front and the back of your hand, and then as you curl your fingers into a fist, do the secret move quickly and smoothly. Then go back to the front of your hand and do another adjustment moving the elastic down to the base of your fingers. This little bit of fiddling helps conceal the maneuvering of your fingers. Just keep all the fiddling casual, and small in nature so the secret move will blend in nicely.

BE SALT

CHAPTER 28

Difficulty Rating: ★★★★ You are hiding things in your hand and moving it secretly to another place. Put in the time and this will play so memorably for your lesson.

Effect: Salt is poured into a tube of paper. It vanishes and later appears in a hand previously shown to be empty.

Connection: The salt is a reminder that Jesus called us to be the salt of the Earth and bring glory to God.

Scripture: Matthew 5:13–16

MATERIALS

- Bible with verse reference marked

- pen with cap

- hot-glue gun

- small plastic cup (such as a medicine cup)*

- paper

- scissors

- salt

* Small plastic cup should be small enough to be concealed in the palm of your hand without showing above or below hand.

PREPARATION

1. Break the clip off of the pen cap so that the rim is even.

2. Use hot-glue gun to secure cap inside the small plastic cup (image a).

A
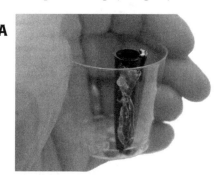

3. Practice the illusion.

SCRIPT

(Read Matthew 5:13–16 aloud.)

You are the salt of the earth. But what good is salt if it has lost its flavor? Can you make it salty again? It will be thrown out and trampled underfoot as worthless.

You are the light of the world–like a city on a hilltop that cannot be hidden. No one lights a lamp and then puts it under a basket. Instead, a lamp is placed on a stand, where it gives light to everyone in the house. In the same way, let your good deeds shine out for all to see, so that everyone will praise your heavenly Father.

(*Cut sheet of paper in half widthwise. Write the word* LIGHT *on one half of the paper.*)

(*Put unused half sheet of paper and scissors away. As you do, conceal the plastic cup in your hand. Pick up the paper with both hands to display the word. This makes your cup-holding hand look more natural.*)

Jesus tells us to be salt and light. What that means is that Jesus wants us to use our life and all the gifts God has given us to bring glory to God.

(*Roll the* LIGHT *paper up with the cup inside. Do not roll so tightly that you can't get the cup out easily. Don't let the audience know the cup is inside. Twist off the bottom of the paper so you have a closed bottom. See image b.*)

B

(*Pour salt into the paper tube, secretly pouring it into the cup. Be careful not to get much salt in the pen cap.*)

What are some ways we can be salt in our world?

(*As the audience responds, pick up the pen and use the flat end to poke the salt down in the tube. Then when you are ready, poke the end of the pen into the cap. See image c.*)

C

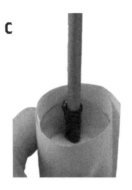

(*Secretly pull the cup of salt out, concealing it behind your palm. See image d.*)

D

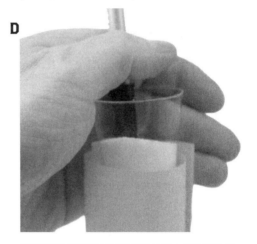

YOUR HAND GOES CLOSE TO THE TOP EDGE OF THE TUBE AS YOU PUT THE PEN AND CUP OUT. THE CUP WILL ALIGN WITH YOUR PALM.

(*Wave the pen over the paper tube. Then turn the tube over—no salt will pour out, to the amazement of the audience. Toss the tube into the audience to be examined.*)

When we lose our saltiness we are not effective in accomplishing God's plans. We won't be able to impact this world for him.

Tip: When holding the pen and secret cup, your hand should look as it would if you were just holding a pen (image e). **Make sure your hand looks relaxed and natural.**

E

```
HAND SHOWN OPEN FOR
EXPLANATION PURPOSES.
IN PERFORMANCE YOUR HAND
WOULD BE CURLED CLOSED.
```

(Show your non-pen-holding hand empty and then transfer the pen and cup to it. See image f.)

F

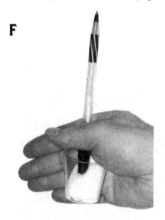

(Keep the cup hidden from view. Then show your other hand empty. Pull the pen out and close your hand around the cup. See images g and h.)

G

H

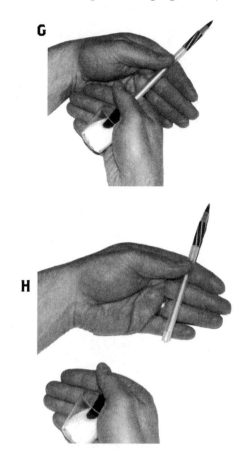

(Wave the pen over the closed hand, and then tip it over and let the salt pour out. Keep your hand closed around the cup so that the audience doesn't see the cup.)

When we make the choice to listen to God's promptings and follow his Word, we will be salty and bring that to a world that desperately needs it.

Let's pray and ask God to make us salty. *(Casually put empty cup in your pocket.)*

CHAPTER 29

NAAMAN THE LEPER

Difficulty Rating: ★★✦ One critical but tricky move.

Effect: A napkin with spots is torn up, soaked in water, fanned, and shown dry and spot-free.

Connection: Illustrates the story of Naaman, but could also be used to demonstrate how forgiveness from Jesus cleanses our soul.

Scripture: 2 Kings 5:1–14

MATERIALS

- Bible with verse reference marked

- 2 identical paper napkins

- marker

- container of water (wide and opaque—not clear; a rectangular container would work well)

- hand fan

PREPARATION

1. Using the marker, draw several spots on one of the napkins.

2. Crumple up the un-spotted napkin.

3. Behind the container of water, place the fan in an open position. Next to that, place the crumpled napkin very close to the container so that it can't be seen from the front (image a).

A

IMAGE SHOWS A ROUND CONTAINER, BUT A RECTANGULAR CONTAINER IS RECOMMENDED.

4. Practice the illusion.

SCRIPT

(*As you perform the illusion, read 2 Kings 5:1–14 directly from Scripture or paraphrase the story to keep it lively. When you mention that Naaman was a leper, hold up the spotted napkin.*) This napkin represents the skin spots associated with the disease known as leprosy. Leprosy is a skin disease that horribly disfigures and hurts the person who has it. Nowadays, there are treatments for leprosy and in most countries, it isn't the problem that it was in Bible times.

(*Tear up the napkin a few times and crumple it up. See image b.*) Elisha said that Naaman would be healed if he dipped himself seven times in the water of the Jordan River.

B

(*Dip the torn spotted napkin in and out of the water container seven times as in the story. While you do, use your other hand to secretly take the dry napkin from behind the water container and hold it in your closed hand.*)

(*After the seventh dip, leave the spotted napkin in the water. Mime that it is still in your hand, by pulling the hand out curled up. Shake your hand a bit, and water will drip off your hand looking as if it is coming from the napkin.*)

(*Then bring the hand holding the dry napkin near the wet one, your dry hand will be closed concealing the napkin. Open the dry hand a bit. While touching the tips of your dry hand, pretend to drop a napkin into it from your wet, empty hand. See image c. Keep the action quick and small. If the audience sees a bit of the dry napkin, it's not a problem.*)

C

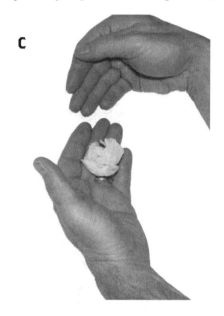

(*Close your dry hand back over the napkin. Immediately use your wet hand to reach for the open fan. Fan the dry, closed hand. Then open your closed hand, and reveal the clean, dry napkin.*)

Naaman followed God's plan and was healed of his spots!

CHAPTER 30

ONE WAY TO HEAVEN

Difficulty Rating: ★★ You have to be flexible with scripting and remember some of the gags.

Effect: This isn't as much an illusion as an object lesson. Although you are giving the illusion that you are dumb and don't know how to blow up a balloon.

Connection: Illustrates that there is only one way to get to Heaven.

Scripture: John 14:6

MATERIALS

- Bible with verse reference marked

- balloons

- permanent marker

PREPARATION

"Everything is practice." —Pele

SCRIPT

Who knows what this is? Just shout it out, you don't have to raise your hands for this. A balloon? Right. What do you do with a balloon? Blow it up? How? (*When the kids shout their replies, just pretend to hear the following suggestions and act on each in turn. Really play it up and have fun!*)

Blow on it? (*Hold on to balloon and blow at it.*)

Put it in my mouth? (*Put the whole thing in your mouth.*) EWWWW! (*Take it out of your mouth and get a new balloon.*)

Just put an end in my mouth and blow? (*Kids yell, "YES!!!" Put the round end in and blow so it blows out of your mouth and drops on the floor. Get another balloon.*)

Use the other end? Oh the one with the hole? Okay . . . (*Put the end in your mouth and blow, but don't hold the balloon so it blows out of your mouth onto the floor again. Get another balloon.*)

Hold it and blow? (*Blow up balloon. Look proud until you release the neck and balloon deflates.*)

Tie a knot? (*Tie balloon in a knot before attempting to blow air in it.*)

Oh, put the knot on AFTER I blow it up? Of course! (*Get another balloon, blow it up, and pretend to tie a knot in it. Then release balloon and let it fly around.*)

(*Get a final balloon, blow it up, and tie it off.*)

This balloon teaches us an important truth from the Bible. John 14:6 tells us Jesus said, "I am the way, the truth, and the life. No one can come to the Father except through me." Jesus was saying that he is the only way to get to Heaven—just like we saw that there is only one way to blow up a balloon. The one way to get to Heaven is through a relationship with Jesus.

(*Use permanent marker to print the name* Jesus *or draw a cross on the balloon.*)

> SIMPLE? YES! IMPACTFUL? YES! I HAVE MADE THIS SIMPLE CONCEPT LAST TWELVE MINUTES, WHICH DRIVES THE KIDS INSANE! AS A RESULT, WHEN YOU GET TO THE LESSON'S POINT IT IS VERY MEMORABLE.

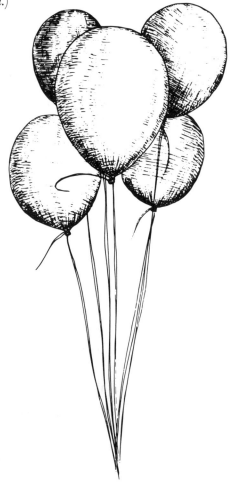

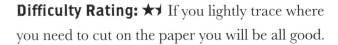
Difficulty Rating: ★↙ If you lightly trace where you need to cut on the paper you will be all good.

Effect: A piece of paper is torn and the piece left forms pictures.

Connection: Illustrates the story of Paul's shipwreck.

Scripture: Acts 27

MATERIALS

- Bible with verse reference marked

- 8.5x8.5-inch (or larger) square of paper

- pen

- scissors

PREPARATION

1. Fold the paper square from the bottom up to the top (image a).

A

2. Fold the right side to the left (image b).

B

3. Fold the top right corner down to the bottom left corner (image c).

C

4. Fold the bottom left corner up to meet the top edge (image d).

D

5. Use a pen or pencil to draw the marks shown in image e. Use a pen or pencil in performance, the Xs indicate sections to be cut off and discarded.

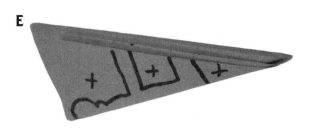
E

6. Practice the illusion.

SCRIPT

(Have someone read Acts 27 from the Bible as you do the cutting. Ask them to pause at the designated points to give you an opportunity to show each shape.)

(As the story begins, begin cutting out the first shape. At verse four, open the paper up to show a ship's steering wheel. See image f. Fold it back up.)

F

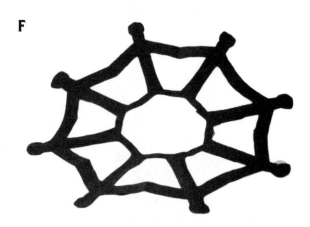

(At verse thirteen, turn the folded paper as shown in image g. Show audience the anchor.)

G

(Then cut the top off the anchor and make a lengthwise cut from the top down. Stop cutting as you near the hooks of the anchor. See image h.)

H

(At verse 44, open paper up to reveal the circle of men whom God spared from the storm. See image i. Break the circle apart to make a string of men.)

I

IMAGE SHOWS PAPER PARTIALLY OPENED. WHEN FULLY OPENED, THERE ARE EIGHT MEN STANDING IN A CIRCLE.

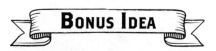
BONUS IDEA

Teach kids to do this as a craft.

CHAPTER 32

PETER ESCAPES PRISON

Difficulty Rating: ★★★★ The secrets behind the illusion aren't difficult, but there are a couple of points at which you have to move at just the right angles to sell the illusion.

> THIS IS MY FAVORITE ILLUSION IN THE BOOK. IF YOU NEVER DO THE ILLUSION, DO THE STORY AT LEAST. IT'S A BLAST!
>
> —RANDY

Effect: A handkerchief is trapped in a glass, but then seemingly melts through the bottom of the glass to become free.

Connection: Illustrates Peter's miraculous escape from prison.

Scripture: Acts 12:1–17

MATERIALS

- Bible with verse reference marked

- Script for this illusion, pages 82–84

- 2 dowels

- tape

- 3 differently colored handkerchiefs

- black thread, several inches

- clear glass

- rubber band

PREPARATION

1. Photocopy the script on pages 82–84.

2. Tape the top edge of the second page to the bottom of the first page, making a long length of paper. Tape additional sheets of paper to the top and bottom, making a length of paper 8.15 inches wide and 44 inches long.

3. Attach the length of paper to two dowels to create a scroll. Wrap the top and bottom sheets around the dowels a few time to secure them before taping.

4. Roll up scroll.

5. Wrap black thread around one corner of a handkerchief. Tie securely (image a). Be sure to secure thread to the handkerchief well as you will be pulling on the thread to release the handkerchief.

A

6. Practice the illusion.

OPTIONAL IDEA

You can read the story straight from Acts 12:1–17 instead of using the scripted version below.

SCRIPT

Back in Bible times, God's special words were recorded on scrolls and read out weekly in the temple. The temple is where God's people met to learn and worship him, just like we do at our church.

(Hold up scroll.) I have a scroll that takes a true story from the Bible and presents it in a playful and profound way. *(Play up the letter P in the story.)*

(Open the scroll and read.)

I would like to propose a little prose about Peter and the power of prayer. Peter proclaimed powerfully the power of God's perfect Son Jesus, and even when other people tried to persuade Peter to stop, he persisted preaching. So King Herod, the pompous president of the people pulled Peter away and put Peter in prison.

(Hold up the glass and explain it is the prison. Show the handkerchief with the secret thread and say that it represents Peter. Place Peter in the bottom of the glass, secretly keeping the thread outside the glass. See image b.)

B

THE THREAD SHOULD ALWAYS FACE YOU.

King Herod proclaimed Peter was to be padlocked to prison guards and placed in a prison cell where no persons were ever paroled.

(Hold up a second handkerchief. Tell audience the second handkerchief represents the guards and place it on top of the Peter handkerchief. See image c.)

C

In fact this pompous president promised to put Peter out of every person's hair by having Peter put out of commission permanently.

(*Take the third handkerchief and place it over the mouth of the glass. Tell the audience that the third handkerchief represents the prison door. Hold up rubber band and explain that it is the lock. Place rubber band over the third handkerchief over the top of the glass trapping the guards and Peter inside the jail cell. See image d.*)

D

IN THE IMAGE, THE THIRD HANDKERCHIEF IS REPLACED WITH CLEAR PLASTIC WRAP SO THAT YOU CAN SEE WHAT WILL BE BENEATH THE HANDKERCHIEF.

This prompted God's people to pray and ask God to provide a way that Peter could be pulled from this prickly, perilous predicament. The people prayed persistently and never gave up. Peter prayed, too, and he had peace in his heart. He had so much peace, Peter was able to have a pleasant night's sleep.

(*Turn the bottom of the glass toward the audience and show the solid bottom and that the handkerchiefs are all trapped inside. See image e. If you crumple the handkerchief around the black thread, it will be concealed.*)

E

It was so quiet you could hear a pin prick a purple peacock—okay that part isn't in the Bible, but next part is!

Suddenly, an angel of God appeared and poked Peter to get Peter awake. Peter was puzzled. He appeared to be perceiving things improperly, or perhaps dreaming. But the angel persisted and proclaimed to Peter, "Get up, put on your sandals and let's blow this popsicle stand!"

"But what about these pile of chains pinning me to the pudgy prison guards of the pompous president of the people?" As soon as Peter posed this question the chains popped off! Peter and his providing angel pal proceeded out of the prison cell. Peter was perspiring as they paraded past all the pudgy prison guards of the pompous president of the people into the prison yard. Once there the huge padlock presented itself.

"Keep pacing forward," persuaded Peter's angel pal and POW the padlock popped off, the prison gate opened, and Peter was free!

(With the glass held mouth up, reach under the glass, grab the thread and pull the Peter handkerchief out of the glass. See images f and g. It will look like you pulled the handkerchief out of the bottom of the glass. Don't let the thread be seen.)

F

G

IMAGE H SHOWS WHAT THE AUDIENCE WILL SEE.

H

(Hold up handkerchief. Then as you describe Peter running off, bounce handkerchief and move from one side to the other as if it is running. Place handkerchief aside or in a pocket.)

Peter ran off and told all the people who had been persistently praying for Peter about the pesky padlock, *(Take rubber band off the glass.)* the prodigious prison doors, *(Remove handkerchief from on top of the glass.)* and the pudgy prison guards *(Take out the handkerchief in the jar.)* and pronounced his freedom! *(Show that the glass is empty, the Peter handkerchief was no longer there.)*

The people all praised God for providing the perfect way for Peter to continue proclaiming the promises of God to the people of this planet. Everyone learned that no matter how big or small a problem they have, God has the power to open any prison door, to help with any pain or problem. We just need to present that problem or pain to God and let the power of prayer provide the answer, just like it did with Peter in prison.

A perfect point to prove positive the power of persistent prayer!

CHAPTER 33
LIFE OF CHRIST IN CARDS

Difficulty Rating: ★★★ You really need to know the story well to keep it flowing and in sync with the cards you deal. As far as moves go, it is easy.

Effect: A deck of cards is shown one at a time, surprisingly illustrating a story being told.

Connection: Illustrates the story of Jesus' life.

Scripture: No specific reference. This illusion is an overview of the gospels.

Note: This works best with an older group of kids who know a little about card suits and card games.

MATERIALS

- deck of playing cards

PREPARATION

1. Arrange the deck of cards in the following order, from the top of the deck down.

A=Ace, K= King, Q=Queen, J=Jack, S=Spades, H=Hearts, D=Diamonds, C=Clubs

AS, QH, JH, JOKER, AD, 2D, 3D, KD, 5H, 6H, 7H, 10S, 2S, 4D, 9C, 7C, 8D, JS, 6C, 4H, 2H, 8H, 4C, 5C, 8S, 8C, JC, 4C, 9H, 9S, 9D, 3S, 3C, 10H, 10D, 10C, 5D, 6D, 7D, KS, KC, 2C, AC, AH, 5S, 6S, 7S, QD, QS, QC, JD, 3H, KH.

2. Practice the illusion.

SCRIPT

(*Turn over the cards indicated as specified in the script.*)

This is the story of a man named Jesus (AS) who was a lowly carpenter's son. Mary (QH) was his mother, and Joseph (JH) was his earthly father.

Jesus wasn't just an ordinary man; he was the Son of God and the sworn enemy of the devil (JOKER). The devil devised three tests with which he tempted Jesus. The first temptation (AD) came after Jesus had been fasting in the wilderness for forty days. The devil tried to get Jesus to turn stones into bread, but Jesus refused and beat that first temptation. The second temptation (2D) had the devil trying to get Jesus to test God. Again, Jesus refused and beat that temptation. The third temptation (3D) was an attempt to get Jesus to worship the devil. Again Jesus beat this temptation.

Jesus was able to resist because he knew what the Bible said and he obeyed it. Jesus was tested and he shone like a king (KD). The devil could do nothing else but RUN away. (5H, 6H, 7H).

Jesus then began his ministry and he started by picking twelve disciples (10S plus 2S). There were fishermen and tax collectors. It was a real ODD group of men (4D, 9C, 7C, and 8D).

Really there were only eleven disciples since one of them, Judas Iscariot (JS) would later betray Jesus. Jesus went around healing the six (6C) . . . I mean "the sick," and helping the unFOR—(4H) TUN—(2H) ATE—(8H).

He also FORced (4C) the money changers from the Temple.

One day he fed 5,000 people (5C) from five loaves and two fish. The people ATE (8S) and ATE (8C) until they were full.

One of the most amazing things Jesus did was raise a man named Lazarus (JC) from the grave, after he had been there four days (4C).

Whenever Jesus came to town he always spoke to a FULL HOUSE (9H, 9S, 9D, 3S, and 3C).

The religious leaders of the day were getting really upset with Jesus and planned to kill him. They needed someone who could get close to Jesus in order for their plan to work. Judas was their man.

The religious leaders approached Judas and offered him thirty pieces of silver (10H, 10D, and 10C) if he would betray Jesus. Judas took the money and betrayed Jesus. When he realized what he had done, he RAN away (5D, 6D, 7D) and killed himself.

Jesus was then taken to the high Priest (KS) and Pilate (KC). Jesus was beaten, whipped, spit on, and laughed at. It was decided that even though he had done nothing wrong, Jesus would be crucified, or hung on a cross to die.

Jesus was put on a cross between two thieves (2C). One of the thieves (AC)

mocked and cursed Jesus. The other one (AH) believed Jesus was the Messiah, the Son of God, and gave his heart to God.

When Jesus was put on the cross to die, his disciples were scared that they would be killed, too. So they RAN away (5S, 6S, 7S). Three women stayed by Jesus during this time. They were Mary Magdalene (QD), Mary the wife of Clopas (QS) who was his mother's sister, and his mother Mary (QC).

Jesus died on that cross. To make sure he was dead the Roman soldier (JD) pierced Jesus side with a sword and more blood was spilt to cover the sins of the world. Jesus was laid in a tomb for three days (3H).

On the third day, Jesus was raised from the dead! He had defeated death, the devil, and sin. He showed the world that he is the King of kings. He is King of hearts (KH). Is he king of your heart?

ENRICHMENT IDEA

To add to this presentation you can cut the deck several times in a way that doesn't disturb the order of the deck. An easy way to do this is to put a good bend in the back corner of the king of hearts. This will make a space in the cards when they are in a pile and make it easy to cut (image a).

A

Here is how to cut the cards to keep the deck from getting mixed up. With the deck face down on the table, cut some cards from the top of the deck (image b) and place them on the table.

B

Take the rest of the deck and place it on top (image c).

C

Because of the bent card (KH) you now know where to cut again, taking the bent card and all the cards above it. Place those face down on the table, and replace the rest of the deck on top. You have cut the cards, restored the cut, and not disturbed the order. Do this a few times in the presentation.

CHAPTER 34

TICKET TO HEAVEN

Difficulty Rating: ★✎ Must remember the folding pattern and where each piece goes in the story.

Effect: A sheet of paper is folded and torn, and the pieces arranged to form pictures.

Connection: Illustrates the story of Jesus' crucifixion.

Additional Scripture:

Romans 10:9–10, John 1:12

Bonus: It could also illustrate a lesson on communion.

MATERIALS

- Bible with Scripture references marked

- 8.5x11-inch sheet of paper

- transparent tape

PREPARATION

1. Fold the top left corner of the sheet of paper down to the bottom right until the top edge is flush with the right edge (image a).

A

2. Take the top right corner and fold to the bottom left until it is flush (images b and c).

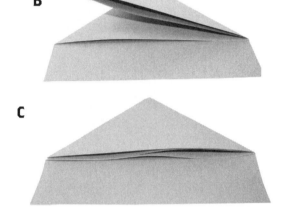

B

C

3. Fold the right side over to the left (image d). This makes your ticket to Heaven!

D

4. If desired, prefold ticket into thirds.

E

5. Practice the illusion.

I would like to tell you the story of two boys, Billy and Willy. They were about the same age as you.

One day Billy and Willy's parents took them to church. The Sunday school teacher was talking about Jesus. She said Jesus was God's Son and that he had died on a cross. She said Jesus died so that people could have their sins forgiven and go to Heaven.

Willy stayed after class and asked his teacher how he could be forgiven and go to Heaven. Willy prayed to God and admitted he was a sinner and that he believed Jesus paid the penalty for his sin. He prayed that he wanted Jesus to be his Lord and Savior. At that moment, Willy became one of God's children and received a ticket to Heaven.

(*Hold up the ticket you prepared.*) This represents a ticket to Heaven.

Billy couldn't believe the change in his brother's life. Willy was happy and he was reading his Bible every day. Willy started doing good things for others, and he didn't even expect a reward for doing it.

Billy wanted to be more like Willy but he figured he didn't need Jesus. He planned to be good enough to get to Heaven all on his own. So Billy tried to be good and obey his parents. He went to Bible club, and tried to read the Bible. Just to make sure he was going to Heaven, Billy took some of his brother's ticket.

(*Tear one-third off the ticket.*)

Willy continued to grow and was telling others about how Jesus had changed his life. But Billy was still missing something. A short time later Billy decided he would get baptized, do at least one good deed a day, and would pray harder. Just to be sure he was doing enough to make it to Heaven, he took some more of his brother's ticket to Heaven.

(*Tear another third off the ticket. See image f.*)

F

One day the family decided to go on a picnic. On the way, they were involved in a car accident and both boys were killed. The next thing Billy knew, he was standing before God. God asked him, "Billy, why should I let you into Heaven?"

Billy said, "Well, I've tried to be good, I've gone to church, I haven't done any major sins like rob a bank or kill someone . . . and I have these pieces of a ticket to Heaven."

God spoke, "Open it up." (*Open the pieces from the first two thirds and shape the word HELL. See image g.*)

G

Billy saw that he didn't have a ticket to Heaven, but instead had a ticket to hell, separation forever from God.

His brother Willy then was standing before God, who asked him, "Willy, why should I let you into Heaven?" Willy responded, "I prayed and asked Jesus to forgive me of my sins and become Lord of my life and he did, and I received a ticket to Heaven."

God spoke, "Open it up." (*Open remaining piece to show the cross. See image h.*)

H

Willy had a ticket to Heaven because of the cross. All the things Billy did to get to Heaven were good things, and things that we should do, too. But doing good things is something we do as a way of expressing our love for God. Good deeds won't get anyone into Heaven.

Believing in what Jesus did on the cross is the only way to get to Heaven. When Willy did that he received the greatest gift. (*Rearrange letters to spell LIFE. See image i.*)

I

Life. Eternal life, life forever with God in Heaven. There is one letter left over, the letter *I*. To choose life, to choose Jesus, is a choice I have to make for me and you have to make for you. A brother, parent, or friend can't do it for you.

If you were to die today and God asked you why he should let you into Heaven what will you say? If you haven't chosen the way of the cross, if you haven't accepted Jesus as your Lord and Savior, you haven't received the gift of life and a ticket to Heaven.

(*Give an invitation for anyone who wants to receive Jesus as their Savior and receive their ticket to Heaven.*)

ENRICHMENT IDEA

(*If you have time, before giving the invitation, follow the additional script below, showing what Jesus did on the cross. After that, close with the invitation.*)

Jesus is our ticket to Heaven. He is God's perfect Son who came to Earth to save us from the punishment for our sin. The religious leaders of the day wanted Jesus dead. Jesus was betrayed, beaten, mocked, and spit on.

Then it was decided they would crucify him. Two thieves were crucified beside Jesus and Jesus' cross was in the middle.

(*Make two smaller crosses on either side of the big cross from pieces of paper. See image j on the next page.*)

They hung a sign above the cross
that said, "King of the Jews".

(*Place large rectangle over the big cross. See image j.*)

Jesus died on that cross and he took
the punishment for our sins. To make
sure he was dead, the Roman guard
pierced Jesus' side with a sword.

(*Place remaining paper next to cross to
represent the sword. See image j.*)

Jesus was laid in a tomb for three days, but
he didn't stay dead. On the third day he was
raised from the dead and appeared to his
disciples and hundreds of people. In doing so
Jesus made it possible for us to go to Heaven.

Which boy represents you in the story?
Do you know what ticket you have?

J

Alternate arrangement of paper pieces:

CHAPTER 35

IN THE LIONS' DEN

Difficulty Rating: ★★★ A concealed secret move and audience management are key. The method is not difficult. Some arts and crafts preparation is required.

Effect: A card is trapped in ropes but breaks free.

Connection: Illustrates the story of Daniel in the lions' den. Could be used to tell any Bible story about being freed from bondage, slavery, or literal chains.

Scripture: Daniel 6

MATERIALS

- Bible with Scripture reference marked
- "Lion Art," page 95
- "Daniel Art," page 96
- cardstock
- 2 6-foot lengths of thin rope
- spool of thread the same color as the rope

PREPARATION

1. Similar to the set up in Chapter 10, Cords of Sin, fold both ropes in half and tie those middles together with a piece of thread (image a). See page 30 as needed for further instruction.

A

2. On cardstock, make two copies of the lion image and one copy of the Daniel image (pp. 95–96).

3. Cut a hole in the middle of the Daniel card.

4. Cut two holes in the top corners of the lion cards.

5. Place the prepared rope out of sight but positioned so that you can easily grab it at the join when needed.

6. Practice the illusion.

PRACTICE TIP

Use 3 chairs to be your volunteers. The cards can sit upright against the back of the chair which will allow you to thread the cards as you will in performance. This way you don't need to have 3 kids around as you rehearse and can still give this the practice it deserves.

SCRIPT

(Select three volunteers to assist you. Two volunteers will hold lion cards and pretend to be lions, and the third will hold the Daniel card and represent Daniel.)

(Read or have another volunteer read Daniel 6 from the Bible, or tell the story in your own words. When you get to the part of Daniel being put in prison, bring out the ropes. As you show the ropes to the audience, cover the join with your hand. Secretly line up the joined section of the rope to the middle of the back of the volunteer Daniel. See image b.)

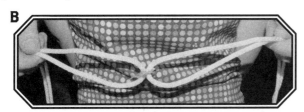

FOR ILLUSTRATIVE PURPOSES, THE THREAD IN THE PHOTO IS THICKER THAN YOU WOULD ACTUALLY USE. IN PERFORMANCE, YOU WOULD USE A SINGLE LOOP OF THREAD ON THE ROPES SO THAT IT WILL BREAK EASILY.

(Bring the four ends of the rope to the front of the volunteer. Thread the ropes through the hole in the middle of the Daniel card. See image c.)

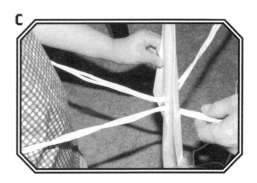

(Have Daniel volunteer press the Daniel card against them and ensure the ropes are snug across their back. See image d.)

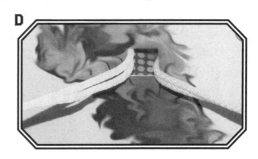

(As you hand the ends of the ropes to each "lion," switch one end so that each lion will have one end of EACH rope in their hand. You have lots of time and cover to do this. See image e.)

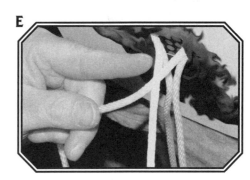

(Thread the lions onto the ropes and bring them towards Daniel. See image f.)

F

LION CARD

DANIEL CARD

FOR CLARITY, THERE SHOULD BE THREE KIDS IN THE PHOTO, BUT I ONLY HAVE TWO DAUGHTERS!

—RANDY

(When, in your reading of the story, you are ready to set Daniel free, subtly break the thread loop as the lion volunteers pull the ends of their ropes and take a big step backwards. The ropes will go "through" the Daniel volunteer and release the Daniel card. The lion cards will stay on the ropes.)

PERFORMANCE TIP

- Stand behind the Daniel volunteer. As you instruct the lions to pull, help the thread break, so that the release happens smoothly. Also, the Daniel card should be held against the child's stomach so that the ropes don't tear the hole as they pass through it. You may want to laminate the cards to make them stronger so they don't easily tear.

- Please be very careful when touching children in your care. Always have a second, non-related adult with you whenever you are working with children.

Instant Bible Lessons: *Gospel Illusions: Object Lessons You Can Do!*

CHAPTER 36

FLOWERFUL

Difficulty Rating: ★★★★ Some arts and crafts, but mainly for the secret moves needed, you want them to be smooth. It isn't as complex as it might read. Try it in front of a mirror and see.

Effect: A lot of colorful tissue paper seeds fly through the air, coming from a seemingly empty tube.

Connection: Illustrates how God made each of us unique and for a purpose.

Scripture: No specific Scripture, though this could be applied to many passages, including one of Jesus' parables.

Note: I wrote this original story to speak into the lives of our special-needs friends. This can be modified for other audiences. Simply change some of the story near the end to reflect a theme of being comfortable in the skin God created us with, accepting our quirks, or feeling like we don't fit in. Feel free to modify this story to suit your needs.

MATERIALS

- Flower Art, page 100

- Butterfly Art, page 101

- scissors

- toilet-paper tube

- transparent tape

- paper towel

- rubber band

- hole punch

- several colors of tissue paper

- hand fan

PREPARATION

1. Make copies of Flower Art (p. 100) and Butterfly Art (p. 101) or draw your own images.

2. Cut a toilet-paper tube to fit in your palm.

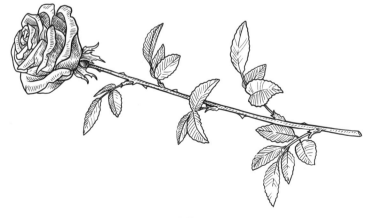

3. Compress one end of the tube and tape the edges, leaving the center open enough that your middle finger fits snugly inside (image a).

A

4. Use a hole punch or scissors to create a lot of colorful tissue-paper confetti.

5. Fill the toilet-paper tube with the confetti

6. Close the open end of the tube by putting a piece of paper towel over it and securing it with a rubber band (image b).

B

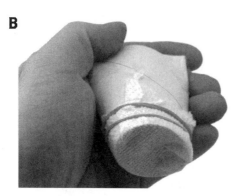

7. Practice the illusion.

SCRIPT

Most of the time, I tell you stories from the Bible. This story is not from the Bible. It is a made-up story called a *parable*. Jesus told parables to teach others about God and his great love for everyone. Just like Jesus' stories, this parable is about God's love for you—just the way you are!

(*Hold up picture of butterfly.*) In a magical land there was a butterfly breed born with a damaged wing, no one can explain why, but as a result the butterflies would fly . . . differently than the other butterflies. Some other insects rejected them, laughing at the "weird" way they flew in the sky, sometimes bumping into a flower here or there, zip-zagging to and fro rather than going from *A* to *B* in a straight line.

These butterflies were feeling pretty low, very down on themselves, and sad. Then one day the Creator of the universe spoke to them. He said, "Beautiful butterflies, you are created with purpose. You have reason. You bring this world a gift. (*Cup your hand around the tube of confetti you prepared. Hold flower picture in front of the tube. Use your middle finger to make sure the top of the tube is pried open. See image c.*)

C

Without you and your so-called funny or irregular flight pattern this breed of flower would not exist. (*Roll flower paper around the tube. See image d.*)

D

(*As you say the following, pick up the fan and open it.*) "Many breeds of insects depend on this flower for food. Without this flower, these insects might die off. The special way you fly allows only you to pollinate the right SEEDS to create this beautiful flower. You are a gift and you bless this world." (*As you say the word seeds, tip the paper tube so that the confetti spills out. Use fan to make the confetti fly!*)

YOU, every one of you in this room, like one of these butterflies. You reflect so amazingly the unconditional love of God, of his grace, acceptance, and beauty. The reality is that you are amazing creations of God and his amazing gifts to this world.

Instant Bible Lessons: *Gospel Illusions: Object Lessons You Can Do!*

CHAPTER 37
SANDS OF TIME

Difficulty Rating: ★★★★ Arts and crafts preparation. Once prepared, it is all about presentation.

Effect: A pile of sand disappears only to appear inside an egg.

Connection: Reminds us to fill the limited number of days in our lives with things of eternal significance.

Scripture: Ephesians 2:10, Psalm 139:16, Psalm 39:4

Additional Scripture: 1 Corinthians 3:10–15 or John 10:10

MATERIALS

- Bible with Scripture references marked

- Double-Walled Bag instructions and materials, beginning on page 12

- 2 uncooked eggs (and a few extra—just in case!)

- sheet of paper

- transparent tape

- sand

- hot-glue gun

- hour glass

- clear glass

- screw driver

PREPARATION

1. Prepare the Double-Walled Bag, following instructions on page 12. Use lots of glue so the pocket is strong.

2. Hollow out an egg following the directions on page 45. Make the hole on top a bit bigger than described.

3. Roll sheet of paper into a small funnel. Once it is small enough to fit in the hole at the top of the egg, tape it to secure (see image).

4. Place paper funnel in the top egg hole and carefully pour sand into the egg.

5. Use hot glue to lightly fill the hole so that the sand doesn't pour out.

6. Place sand-filled egg in the Double-Walled Bag.

7. Pour about ¼ cup of sand into the clear glass.

8. Practice the illusion.

SANDS OF TIME

SCRIPT

(*Hold up a normal egg.*) An egg is a symbol of life. We each have one life to live. The question is, when you are old and look back at what you have done with your life, what will you see?

(*Crack the egg and drop the yolk into a clear glass.*) For your life to count, it needs to be built on the right foundation, a foundation that gives life. Jesus gives us that foundation and life.

(*Hold up the hour glass.*) This records a certain period of time, as the sands slip through, seconds, and then minutes go by. Each of us only has so many seconds, minutes, hours, days, years to live. Psalm 39:4 tells us, "LORD, remind me how brief my time on earth will be. Remind me that my days are numbered—how fleeting my life is."

God knows the day of our birth and of our death. God wants us to fill our time, our life, with choices and activities that accomplish his plans for us. He wants us to complete the works he has had planned for us from the beginning of time.

Did you know God has plans for you? Psalm 139:16 says, "You saw me before I was born. Every day of my life was recorded in your book. Every moment was laid out before a single day had passed." And Ephesians 2:10 tells us, "We are God's masterpiece. He has created us anew in Christ Jesus, so we can do the good things he planned for us long ago."

Each day the sands of time tick by . . .

(*Take the glass and pour the sand into the secret pocket of the paper bag. Then reach in and take out the egg.*)

One day the last of the sand will run out . . . (*Tear open the FRONT of the bag showing the sand is gone.*)

And one question will remain: as God's servants, have we done a good job serving him and his people? Did we spend our lives living for God?

(*Show the sand-filled egg.*) You are young. You have lots of sand—or time—left in your life, so much potential for what you can do for God. How are you going to spend it?

(*Take the screw driver and chip away the glue, making it look as if you are poking a new hole. Pour the sand out of the egg back into the clear glass.*)

CHAPTER 38

TRANSFORMED

Difficulty Rating: ★★★★★ Lots of precision and many rehearsals are needed to make this illusion convincing and smooth.

Effect: An adult is wrapped in a sheet. When unwrapped, the adult has turned into a child.

Connection: Illustrates the idea of transformation and how all followers of Christ become new creatures.

Scripture: 2 Corinthians 5:17, Romans 12:2

MATERIALS

- Bible with Scripture references marked

- table

- tablecloth

- large blanket or another tablecloth

PREPARATION

1. Well ahead of time, arrange for a child and an adult to assist you with this illusion. You will practice with your volunteers to prepare the illusion. Choose volunteers who are not too dissimilar in height.

2. Cover table with a tablecloth that goes all the way to the floor.

3. Before audience arrives, have the child crouch under the tablecloth-covered table. Put the large blanket folded on top of the table.

4. Practice the illusion.

SCRIPT

Raise your hand if you know what the word *transformation* means. (*Audience responds.*) Transformation means something takes on a new form. It changes into something completely different! The Bible talks a lot about transformation. For example, in 2 Corinthians 5:17 the Bible tells us, "This means that anyone who belongs to Christ has become a new person. The old life is gone; a new life has begun!"

Romans 12:2 goes even further. This verse says, "Don't copy the behavior and customs of this world, but let God transform you into a new person by changing the way you think. Then you will learn to know God's will for you, which is good and pleasing and perfect."

Let's see what transforming into a new person might look like.

Ask for some volunteers and select your accomplice, but make it look random. In nature, God gave us a wonderful illustration of transformation. How many of you know what a caterpillar transforms into? (*Audience responds. Ask the adult volunteer to get down on floor and crawl towards you, like a caterpillar. Volunteer*

should act a bit confused about the directions, so actions will not come across as rehearsed.)

(Take the blanket off the table and open it up so it is in front of you, with it touching the floor and the left edge still flush with the edge of the table. The adult worms their way to you and under the edge of the blanket. Adult then moves to the table, signaling the child to crawl out and lay next to the blanket, as adult takes cover under the table. As all this is going on, talk about caterpillars transforming into butterflies and how they first form a cocoon.)

(Ask the child to move forward with you–still staying behind the blanket–as you move a bit away from the table area. Lay the blanket over the child. Proceed to wrap the child in the blanket explaining to the audience that it is the cocoon.)

(On your signal, the child stands up and comes out of the "cocoon.")

Ta Daa!

Scriptural Index

Old Testament

SCRIPTURAL INDEX

About the Author

Randy has traveled to hundreds of churches, spoken at hundreds of camps, and served as a children's pastor for twenty-five years. He currently serves in Canada's largest Evangelical church, Centre Street Church, where he oversees kindergarten through fourth-grade children and their families. He is also a professional illusionist, having performed thousands of shows for over twenty-five years.

Randy is happily married and has two daughters who joined his family through adoption. Look for a photo of Randy and his daughters in Chapter 35.